The Legacy of the Prophet

Peace Be Upon Him

Stories of the Prophets	ISBN 9781503388406
Seerah of Prophet Muhammad	ISBN 9781094860213
Stories of the Koran	ISBN 9781095900796
Great Women in Islam	ISBN 9781505398304
The Path to Guidance	ISBN 9781643540818
The Battles of the Prophet	ISBN 9781092642507
The Purification of the Soul	ISBN 9781643541389
Tafseer Ibn Kathir	ISBN 9781512266573
Kalid Ibn Al-Walid	ISBN 9781508435204
The Ideal Muslimah	ISBN 9781799015598
Al-Fawaid: Wise Sayings	ISBN 9781727812718
The Book of Hajj	ISBN 9781072243335
40 Hadith Qudsi	ISBN 9781070655949
40 Hadith Nawawi	ISBN 9781070547428

THE AUTHOR

Ḥāfiẓ Abū'l-Faraj ibn Rajab al-Ḥanbalī

He is the Imām and Hāfiẓ, Zaynu'l-Dīn 'Abdur-Raḥmān ibn Aḥmad ibn 'Abdir-Raḥmān ibn al-Ḥasan ibn Muḥammad ibn Abū-l-Barakāt Mas'ūd al-Sulamī al-Ḥanbalī al-Dimashqī. His agnomen was Abū'l-Faraj, and his nickname was Ibn Rajab, which was the nickname of his grandfather who was born in that month.

He was born in Baghdād in 736H and was raised by a knowledgeable and pious family. He died on a Monday night, the fourth of Ramaḍān, 795H in al-Ḥumariyyah, Damascus.

He learned and took knowledge from the greatest scholars of his time. In Damascus, he studied under Ibn Qayyim al-Jawziyyah, Zaynu'l-Dīn al-'Irāqī, ibn al-Naqīb, Muḥammad ibn Ismā'īl al-Khabbāz, Dāwūd ibn Ibrāhīm al-'Aṭṭār, ibn Qāṭī al-Jabal and Aḥmad ibn 'Abdu-l-Hādī al-Ḥanbalī. In Makkah, he heard from al-Fakhr 'Uthmān ibn Yūsuf al-Nuwayrī. In Jerusalem, he heard from al-Ḥāfiẓ al-'Alā'ī. In Egypt, he heard from Ṣadru'l-Dīn Abū'l-Fatḥ al-Maydūmī and Nāṣiru'l-Dīn ibn al-Mulūk.

Many students of knowledge came to him to study under him. Amongst the most famous of his students were: Abū'l-'Abbās Aḥmad ibn Abū Bakr ibn 'Alī al-Ḥanbalī; Abū'l-Faḍl Aḥmad ibn Naṣr ibn Aḥmad; Dāwūd ibn Sulaymān al-Mawsilī; 'Abdu'l-Raḥmān ibn Aḥmad ibn Muḥammad al-Muqrī'; Zaynū'l-Dīn 'Abdu'l-Raḥmān ibn Sulaymān ibn Abū'l-Karam; Abū Dharr al-Zarkashī; al-Qāḍī 'Alā'ū'l-Dīn ibn al-Lahām al-Ba'lī; and Aḥmad ibn Ṣayfū'l-Dīn al-Ḥamawī.

Ibn Rajab devoted himself to knowledge and spent the vast majority of his time researching, writing, authoring, teaching, and giving legal rulings.

Many scholars praised him for his vast knowledge, asceticism and expertise in the Ḥanbalī school of thought. Ibn Qāḍī Shuhbah said of him, 'He read and became proficient in the various fields of science. He engrossed himself with the issues of the madhhab until he mastered it. He devoted himself to the occupation of knowledge of the texts, defects and meanings of the ḥadīth.'[1]

Ibn Ḥajr said of him, 'He was highly proficient in the science of ḥadīth in terms of the names of reporters, their biographies, their paths of narration and awareness of their meanings.'[2]

Ibn Mufliḥ said of him, 'He is the Shaykh, the great scholar, the Ḥāfiẓ, the ascetic, the Shaykh of the Ḥanbalī madhhab and he authored many beneficial works.'[3]

---

[1] Ibn Qāḍī al-Shuhbah, *Tārīkh*, vol. 3, p. 195.

[2] ibn Ḥajr, *Inbā'u'l-Ghamr*, vol. 1, p. 460.

[3] *al-Maqṣad al-Arshad*, vol. 2, p. 81.

He wrote many beneficial works, some of them outstanding such as *al-Qawā'id al-Kubrā fi'l-Furū'* about which it was said, 'It is one of the wonders of this age.'[4] His commentary to at-Tirmidhī is said to be the most extensive and best ever written so much so that al-'Irāqī; about whom ibn Ḥajr said, 'He was the wonder of his age'; would ask for his help when compiling his own commentary to the same book.

- Moreover he has many valuable monographs explaining various aḥādīth such as: *Sharḥ Ḥadith Mā Dhi'bāni Jāi'ān Ursilā fi Ghanam*; *Ikhtiyār al-Awlā Sharḥ Ḥadith Ikhtiṣām al-Mala' al-A'lā*; *Nūr al-Iqtibās fi Sharḥ Waṣiyyah al-Nabī li ibn 'Abbās*; and *Kashfu'l-Kurbah fi Wasfi Ḥāli Ahli-l-Ghurbah.*

- In exegesis his works include: *Tafsir Sūrah al-Ikhlāṣ*, *Tafsir Sūrah al-Fātiḥah*; *Tafsir Sūrah al-Naṣr*, and *al-Istighnā' bi'l-Qur'ān.*

- In ḥadīth his works include: *Sharḥ 'Ilal al-Tirmidhī*; *Fatḥu'l-Bāri Sharḥ Ṣaḥiḥ al-Bukhārī*; and *Jāmi' al-'Ulūm wa'l-Ḥikam.*

- In fiqh his works include: *al-Istikhrāj fi Aḥkām al-Kharāj*; and *al-Qawā'id al-Fiqhiyyah.*

- In biographies his works include the monumental *Dhayl 'alā Ṭabaqāti'l-Ḥanābilah.*

- In exhortation his works include: *Laṭā'if al-Ma'ārif* and *al-Takhwīf min al-Nār.*

---

[4] ibn 'Abdu'l-Hādī, *Dhayl 'alā Ṭabaqāt ibn Rajab*, p. 38.

INTRODUCTION

With the Name of Allāh, the All-Merciful, the Most Merciful

All praise is due to Allāh, Lord of the worlds, a pure and blessed praise as our Lord loves and is pleased with, a praise that behoves the nobility of His face and accords with His magnificence. May Allāh's peace and blessings be upon Muḥammad, the Unlettered Prophet, his family and his Companions.

Imām Aḥmad records the ḥadīth of Ḥanash al-Ṣana'ānī on the authority of ibn 'Abbās who said, 'I was sitting behind the Prophet (ﷺ) when he said, "Young lad, should I not teach you some words through which Allāh will occasion benefit for you?" I said, "Of course!" He said, "Safeguard Allāh and He will safeguard you. Safeguard Allāh and you will find Him in front of you. Know Allāh in times of ease and He will know you in times of hardship. When you ask, ask Allāh. When you seek aid, turn to Allāh. The Pen has dried (after having written) all that will occur. If the whole of creation, in its entirety, was to try and effectuate some benefit for you through something that Allāh has not ordained, they would not be able to do so; and if they wished to harm you through something that Allāh has not decreed, they would not be able to do so. Know that great good lies in bearing with patience what you dislike, that victory comes with patience, that relief comes with distress, and that with hardship comes ease.'"[1]

This is how he related it via the route of Ḥanash along with two other isnāds that are munqaṭi', he mentioned that he did not differentiate the wordings of the various routes in this particular instance.

He also records it via the route of Ḥanash alone, summarised, with the wording, "Young lad, I will relate some words to you: Safeguard Allāh and He will safeguard you. Safeguard Allāh and you will find Him before you. When you ask, ask Allāh. When you seek aid, turn to Allāh. The Pens have been lifted and the books have dried. If the nation were to come in order to benefit you with something that Allāh has not decreed for you, they would not be able to; and if they desired to harm you with something that Allāh has not decreed for you, they would not be able to."[2]

A similar wording was recorded by Tirmidhī, "I will teach you some words: Safeguard Allāh and He will safeguard you. Safeguard Allāh and you will find Him before you. Know that if the nation came together in order to benefit you with something, they would not be able to do so except with something that Allāh has already decreed for you; and were they to come together in

[1] Aḥmad #2803 and it is ṣaḥīḥ

[2] Aḥmad #2669-2763 and it is ṣaḥīḥ

order to harm you with something, they would not be able to do so except with something that Allāh has already decreed against you. The Pens have been lifted and the scrolls have dried."[3]

Ḥāfiẓ Abū 'Abdullāh ibn Mandah said, 'This ḥadīth has various routes from ibn 'Abbās and this is the most authentic of them... this isnād is well-known and its narrators are trustworthy and precise.'

I say: This ḥadīth has been reported by a group of narrators from ibn 'Abbās. Amongst them are his son, 'Alī, and 'Aṭā'[4] and 'Ikrimah.[5] It is also reported from him by 'Umar, the freed-slave of Ghufrah,[6] and 'Abdu'l-Malik ibn 'Umayr[7] and ibn Abī Mulaykah[8] although it is said that they did not hear (ḥadīth) from him. All these isnāds are problematic and some contain additional wordings and others omit some wordings.

The fact that the Prophet (ﷺ) gave this counsel to ibn 'Abbās has also been related from 'Alī ibn Abī Ṭālib,[9] Abū Sa'īd al-

---

[3] Tirmidhī #2516 who said it was ḥasan ṣaḥīḥ

[4] 'Abd ibn Ḥumayd #634 (*Muntakhab*), Ṭabarānī, *al-Kabir* #11416

[5] Ṭabarānī, *al-Kabir* #11560

[6] Ṭabarānī, *al-Kabir* #11560

[7] Ḥākim #6303

[8] Ṭabarānī, *al-Kabir* #11243

[9] Qāḍī Tinnawkhī, *al-Faraj ba'd al-Shiddah*, vol. 1, pg. 112

Khudrī,[10] Sahl ibn Sa'd[11] and other Companions.[12] The isnāds of all these are also problematic. 'Uqaylī mentioned that all the isnāds of the ḥadīth are weak (*layyin*) with some being better than others.[13]

I say: the best of these isnāds is the narration of Ḥanash on the authority of ibn 'Abbās that we have previously mentioned, it is a ḥasan isnād, having nothing untoward in it. We have discussed the various routes of this ḥadīth in detail in *Sharḥ al-Tirmidhī*; our purpose here, however, is to explain the meaning of the ḥadīth and to expound upon its wordings.

This ḥadīth comprises pieces of advice of paramount importance and universal principles that deal with the greatest and most noble aspects of this religion. This is true to such an extent that Imām Abū'l-Faraj in his work, *Ṣayd al-Khāṭir*, said, 'I pondered this ḥadīth and it struck me with awe; I was so astounded that I almost became light headed.' Then he said, 'The prevailing ignorance of this ḥadīth and the lack of understanding thereof is truly distressing!'[14]

---

[10] Abū Ya'lā #1099

[11] Qāḍī Tinnawkhī, *al-Faraj ba'd al-Shiddah*, vol. 1, pg. 112. Suyūṭī, *al-Durr al-Manthūr*, vol. 1, pg. 159 references it to Dāruquṭnī, *Afrād*, ibn Mardawayh, Bayhaqī and Aṣbahānī.

[12] Such as 'Abdullāh ibn Ja'far as recorded ibn Abū 'Āṣim, *al-Sunnah* #315

[13] 'Uqaylī, *al-Du'afā' al-Kabīr*, vol. 3, pg. 54
Refer to Appendix 1 for a sourcing of the various narrations of the ḥadīth.

[14] al-Qārī, *Sharḥ Mishkāt*, vol. 9, pg. 161, said, "'*I was sitting behind the Prophet*(ﷺ),"

=

=

this indicates that (ibn 'Abbās) memorised the incident accurately, brought the words to mind, and accurately conveyed them. This is one of the ḥadīths that he heard from the Messenger of Allāh (ﷺ) directly for most of what he narrates is via the medium of another narrator, however these are taken as proof because they are the mursal narrations of a Companion (which are accepted). The reason for this is that he was very young during the time of the Prophet (ﷺ). The author (Baghawī) said that he was born three years before the Hijra and he was thirteen years old when the Prophet (ﷺ) passed away, some said that he was fifteen at the time and yet others said he was ten. However, he became a great scholar, the ocean of knowledge of this nation because the Prophet (ﷺ) supplicated that he acquire wisdom, understanding and correct interpretation. He saw Jibrīl twice and he became blind at the end of his life. He passed away at Ṭā'if in the year 68H during the rule of ibn al-Zubayr at the age of seventy one. A large number of Companions and Successors narrate from him. *"Young lad,"* the point behind the address is that ibn 'Abbās direct his attention to him and pay heed to what is said. *"Shall I teach you some words,"* points of advice through which you may repress affliction and promote benefit and blessings.'

CHAPTER ONE

Safeguarding Allāh

The saying of the Messenger of Allāh (ﷺ), "Safeguard Allāh and He will safeguard you," means to safeguard the limits of Allāh, His rights, His commands and His prohibitions. These are preserved by meeting His commands with compliance, His prohibitions with avoidance, and His limits by not overstepping or transgressing them such that one leaves what has been prescribed and encroaches on the proscribed.

Hence this sentence covers the performance of all obligations and the abandonment of all prohibitions just as is mentioned in the ḥadīth of Abū Tha'labah that the Prophet (ﷺ) said, "Allāh has obligated various duties so do not be lax in them, He has prohibited various things so do not encroach on them, and He has set limits so do not transgress them."[1]

[1] Dāruquṭnī, vol. 4, pg. 183 #4396, Ṭabarānī, *al-Kabir*, vol. 22, pg. 221
Ibn Ḥajr, *al-Maṭālib al-'Āliyah* #2951 said that its narrators were *thiqah* but that it was munqaṭi'. Nawawī, *al-Arba'īn* #30 ruled it ḥasan as did Sama'ānī, *al-Amālī* as stated by ibn Rajab, *Jāmi' al-'Ulūm*, vol. 2, pg. 150. Albānī and Arna'ūṭ both declared the ḥadīth ḥasan due to supporting witnesses in their respective notes to *Sharḥ al-Ṭaḥāwiyyah.*

All of the above is included in the term, 'preserving the limits of Allāh' and as such is subsumed by the sayings of Allāh,

وَٱلۡحَٰفِظُونَ لِحُدُودِ ٱللَّهِۗ

"...those who preserve the limits of Allāh"[2]

هَٰذَا مَا تُوعَدُونَ لِكُلِّ أَوَّابٍ حَفِيظٖ
﴿٣٢﴾ مَّنۡ خَشِيَ ٱلرَّحۡمَٰنَ بِٱلۡغَيۡبِ وَجَآءَ بِقَلۡبٖ مُّنِيبٍ ﴿٣٣﴾

"This is what you were promised; it is for every penitent and heedful one: those who fear the All-Merciful in the Unseen[3] and come with a contrite heart."[4]

The term, *heedful one* in this verse has been explained to mean one who safeguards the commandments of Allāh[5] and it has also been explained to mean a person whose solicitude for his sins leads him to repent and desist.[6] The verse encompasses both meanings[7] and, moreover, anyone who safeguards the legacy of

---

[2] *al-Tawbah* (9): 112

[3] Or: **"...those who fear the All-Merciful in secret..."**

[4] *Qāf* (50): 32-33

[5] The exegesis of Qatādah as recorded by Ṭabarī

[6] The exegesis of Sa'īd ibn Sinān as recorded by Bayhaqī; ibn 'Abbās, Sa'īd ibn al-Musayyab, Mujāhid and 'Ubayd ibn 'Umayr as recorded by Ṭabarī. cf. Suyūṭī, *al-Durr al-Manthūr*

[7] as stated by Ṭabarī and others.

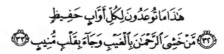

Allāh to His servants and follows it is also included within the scope of the verse. All of these aspects revolve around one and the same fundamental meaning.

One of the wordings of the ḥadīth concerning the Day of Increase in Paradise mentions that "when Allāh, Most High, will summon the inhabitants of Paradise to visit Him, and after He has removed the veils for them, He will say, 'Welcome O servants of Mine: those who safeguarded my legacy, tended to My covenant and feared Me in secret; those who, in every circumstance, remained in dread of Me.'"[8]

Therefore his (ﷺ) commanding ibn 'Abbās to safeguard Allāh comprises all that has been mentioned above.

---

[8] Ibn Abī al-Dunyā, *Ṣifatu'l-Jannah*, pg. 53 and Abū Nu'aym, *Ṣifatu'l-Jannah*, pg. 411.

Mundhirī, *al-Targhīb*, vol. 4, pg. 307 said that it was munkar as a ḥadīth of the Prophet (ﷺ). Ibn Kathīr, *al-Bidāyah wa'l-Nihāyah*, vol. 2, pg. 520 said, 'This is mursal ḍa'īf gharīb, the best that one can say about it is that it is the words of one of the Salaf which were mistakenly attributed to the Prophet (ﷺ). Allāh knows best.' Ibn al-Qayyim, *Ḥādī al-Arwāḥ*, pg. 233 said that it was not authentic as a ḥadīth of the Prophet (ﷺ).

1.1 Safeguarding the Prayers

One of the greatest of matters that require safeguarding is the five daily prayers. Allāh, Most High, says,

حَـٰفِظُواْ عَلَى ٱلصَّلَوَٰتِ وَٱلصَّلَوٰةِ ٱلْوُسْطَىٰ

"Safeguard the prayers - especially the middle one."[9]

وَٱلَّذِينَ هُمْ عَلَىٰ صَلَاتِهِمْ يُحَافِظُونَ

"...those who safeguard their prayer."[10]

The Prophet (ﷺ) said, "Whoever safeguards them has a promise from Allāh that He will grant him entry into Paradise."[11]

Another ḥadīth has, "Whoever safeguards them, they will be a light, a proof and a deliverance for him on the Day of Rising."[12]

---

[9] *al-Baqarah* (2): 238

[10] *al-Ma'ārij* (70): 34

[11] Mālik #268, Abū Dāwūd #425, Nasā'ī #462, ibn Mājah #1401.
It was ruled ṣaḥīḥ by ibn Ḥibbān #1732-2417, ibn 'Abdu'l-Barr, *al-Tamhid*, vol. 5, pg. 187, Nawawī, *Khulāṣatu'l-Aḥkām* #1859, and Albānī, *Ṣaḥīḥ al-Targhib* #370

[12] Aḥmad #6576, Ṭabarānī, *al-Awsaṭ* #1788
It was ruled ṣaḥīḥ by ibn Ḥibbān #1467 and 'Irāqī, *Ṭarḥ al-Tathrib*, vol. 2, pg. 147. Mundhirī, *al-Targhib*, vol. 1, pg. 264 said the isnād was jayyid as did Dhahabī, *Tanqīḥ al-Taḥqiq*, vol. 1, pg. 300. Haythamī, vol. 1, pg. 292 said, 'The narrators of Aḥmad are thiqah.' Arna'ūṭ said that the isnād was ḥasan in his notes to the Musnad and ṣaḥīḥ in his notes to ibn Ḥibbān.

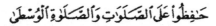

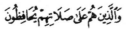

1.2 Safeguarding Purification

The same applies to purification for it is the key to prayer.[13] The Prophet (ﷺ) said, "None safeguards the ablution save a believer."[14]

This is because a servant could well invalidate his state of purification without even being aware of it, therefore safeguarding the state of ablution for prayer is a proof that faith has settled firmly in the heart.

1.3 Safeguarding Oaths

Amongst the things that Allāh has commanded to safeguard is oaths. When He mentioned the expiation of breaking oaths, He said,

ذَٰلِكَ كَفَّٰرَةُ أَيْمَٰنِكُمْ إِذَا حَلَفْتُمْ وَٱحْفَظُوٓا۟ أَيْمَٰنَكُمْ

"That is the expiation for breaking oaths when

[13] As mentioned in the ḥadīth recorded by Tirmidhī #3 on the authority of 'Alī that the Prophet (ﷺ) said, "The key to prayer is purification, it is made inviolable by the *takbīr* and violable by the *taslīm*." He also records this ḥadīth [#4] on the authority of Jābir and [#238] on the authority of Abū Sa'īd al-Khudrī.

[14] Aḥmad #22378-22414-22433-22436, ibn Mājah #277, Dārimī #655 on the authority of Thawbān.

It was ruled ṣaḥīḥ by Suyūṭī, *al-Jāmi' al-Ṣaghīr* #994 and Mundhirī quoted 'Iraqī ruling it ḥasan in his *Amālī*, Arna'ūṭ and ṣaḥīḥ li ghayrihī by Albānī, *Ṣaḥīḥ al-Targhīb* #197-379

you have sworn them. Keep your oaths."[15]

People frequently make oaths and the consequences of breaching them vary: sometimes it will be the expiation for breaking oaths, other times a severe expiation is required (*kaffārah mughallaẓa*), and at other times it requires divorce or the likes to take effect. Faith has entered the heart of a person who takes care of his oaths.

The Salaf would carefully safeguard their oaths. Some of them would never take an oath by Allāh, others would be so guarded that they would give expiation for oaths they thought they may have broken. Imām Aḥmad, on his death bed, enjoined that the expiation for breaking an oath be given saying, 'I think I might have broken an oath that I made.'

It is reported that when Ayyūb (*'alayhis-salām*) passed by any two people swearing an oath by Allāh, he would go and give expiation on their behalf lest they sin without realising. This is why when he made an oath to lash his wife one hundred time, Allāh granted him leeway[16] because of his safeguarding his oaths and the oaths of others. The scholars have differed as to whether this leeway applies to others besides Ayyūb.

Yazīd ibn Abī Ḥabīb said, 'It has reached me that, amongst the Carriers of the Throne, there is one whose eyes shed tears that flow like rivers. Then when he raises his head, he says, "Glory be to You, You are not feared as befits You." Allāh says, "Yet those

[15] *al-Mā'idah* (5): 89

[16] Mentioned in His saying, **"Take a bundle of rushes in your hand and strike with that and do not break your oath."** [*Ṣād* (38): 44]

who make oaths in My name falsely do not know this!'"

A severe threat has been recorded concerning taking false oaths. Frequent oaths in the name of Allāh, or false oaths in His name, arise from ignorance of Allāh and lack of reverence in the heart.

1.4 Safeguarding the Head and Stomach

Some of the things that the believer must safeguard are his head and stomach. Ibn Mas'ūd reports that the Messenger of Allāh (ﷺ) said, "Being shy before Allāh as is truly deserving is to safeguard the head and what it retains and the stomach and what it contains." It is recorded by Aḥmad and Tirmidhī.[17]

Safeguarding the head and what it retains includes safeguarding the hearing, seeing and tongue from falling into the prohibited. Safeguarding the stomach and what it contains includes safeguarding the heart from persisting in the proscribed. Allāh has mentioned all of this in His saying,

إِنَّ السَّمْعَ وَالْبَصَرَ وَالْفُؤَادَ كُلُّ أُولَٰئِكَ كَانَ عَنْهُ مَسْئُولًا ﴿٣٦﴾

"The hearing, the sight and the heart - each of these will be questioned."[18]

Safeguarding the stomach and what it contains includes safe-

[17] Aḥmad #3671, Tirmidhī #2458
Tirmidhī said the ḥadīth was gharīb and Arna'ūt said the isnād was ḍa'īf. Albānī, *Ṣaḥiḥ al-Targhib* #1724-2638-3337 ruled it ḥasan li ghayrihī.

[18] *al-Isrā'* (17): 36

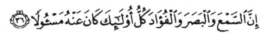

guarding it from consuming unlawful food and drink.

1.5 Safeguarding the Tongue and Private Parts

It is also obligatory to safeguard the tongue and private parts from infringing on the proscribed. Abū Hurayrah reports that the Prophet (ﷺ) said, "Whoever safeguards what is between his jaws and what is between his legs will enter Paradise." It is recorded by Ḥākim.[19]

Bukhārī also records it on the authority of Sahl ibn Sa'd from the Prophet (ﷺ) with the wording, "Whoever guarantees me what is between his jaws and legs, I will guarantee him Paradise."[20]

Aḥmad has the ḥadīth of Abū Mūsā that the Prophet (ﷺ) said, "Whoever safeguards what is between his jaws and his private parts will enter Paradise."[21]

Allāh, Most High, has specifically ordered the safeguarding of the privates and has praised those who do so,

---

[19] Ḥākim #8058 and he said it was ṣaḥīḥ with Dhahabī agreeing.
A ḥadīth of similar meaning is also recorded by Tirmidhī #2409 who said it was ḥasan ṣaḥīḥ and ibn Ḥibbān #5703 on the authority of Abū Hurayrah with the words, "Whoever Allāh protects from the evil of what is between his two lips and between his two legs will enter Paradise."

[20] Bukhārī #6474-6807

[21] Aḥmad #19559, Ḥākim #8063
Arna'ūṭ said that it was ṣaḥīḥ li ghayrihī

قُل لِّلْمُؤْمِنِينَ يَغُضُّوا مِنْ أَبْصَٰرِهِمْ وَيَحْفَظُوا فُرُوجَهُمْ

"Say to the believers that they should lower their eyes and guard their private parts."[22]

وَٱلْحَٰفِظِينَ فُرُوجَهُمْ وَٱلْحَٰفِظَٰتِ

"...men and women who guard their private parts..."[23]

وَٱلَّذِينَ هُمْ لِفُرُوجِهِمْ حَٰفِظُونَ ﴿٥﴾ إِلَّا عَلَىٰٓ أَزْوَٰجِهِمْ أَوْ مَا مَلَكَتْ أَيْمَٰنُهُمْ فَإِنَّهُمْ غَيْرُ مَلُومِينَ ﴿٦﴾

"...those who guard their private parts - except from their wives or those they own (as slaves), in which case they are not blameworthy..."[24]

It is reported that Abū Idrīs al-Khawlānī said, 'When Ādam descended to earth, the first thing that Allāh enjoined upon him was the safeguarding of the privates and that he should only ever put them in that which was lawful.'

---

[22] *al-Nūr* (24): 30

[23] *al-Aḥzāb* (33): 35

[24] *al-Mu'minūn* (23): 5-6

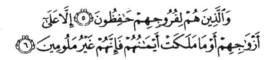

CHAPTER TWO

He will safeguard You

His (ﷺ) saying, "He will safeguard you," means that whoever safeguards the limits of Allāh and tends to the rights due Him, Allāh will safeguard him. This is because the recompense is of the same type as the deed. Allāh, Most High, says,

وَأَوْفُوا بِعَهْدِي أُوفِ بِعَهْدِكُمْ

> **"Honour My contract and I will honour your contract..."**[1]

فَاذْكُرُونِي أَذْكُرْكُمْ

> **"Remember Me - I will remember you."**[2]

إِن تَنصُرُوا اللَّهَ يَنصُرْكُمْ

> **"...if you help Allāh, He will help you..."**[3]

---

[1] *al-Baqarah* (2): 40

[2] *al-Baqarah* (2): 152

[3] *Muḥammad* (47): 7

Allāh's safeguarding His servant is of two types:

1. His safeguarding him in that which would benefit him in his worldly life such as His protecting his body, children, family and wealth.

Ibn 'Umar reports that the Messenger of Allāh (ﷺ) never left saying the following supplication when he awoke and when he went to sleep, "O Allāh, I ask You for well-being in this world and in the Hereafter. O Allāh, I ask You for pardon and well-being in my religion, my worldly life, my family and my wealth. O Allāh, cover my faults and dispel my fears, safeguard me against what is before me and behind me, what is to my right and to my left, and what is above me. I take refuge with Your grandeur lest I be seized from beneath me." The ḥadīth was recorded by Aḥmad, Abū Dāwūd, Nasā'ī and ibn Mājah.[4]

This supplication is derived from His saying,

لَهُۥ مُعَقِّبَٰتٌ مِّنۢ بَيْنِ يَدَيْهِ وَمِنْ خَلْفِهِۦ يَحْفَظُونَهُۥ
مِنْ أَمْرِ ٱللَّهِ

"Everyone has a succession [of Angels] in front of him and behind him, guarding him by Allāh's command."[5]

---

[4] Aḥmad #4785, Abū Dāwūd #5074, Nasā'ī #5531-5532, ibn Mājah #3871. It was declared ṣaḥīḥ by ibn Ḥibbān #961, Ḥākim #1902 with Dhahabī agreeing, Albāni, *Ṣaḥīḥ al-Targhīb* #659, and Arna'ūṭ et. al. Ibn Ḥajr said it was ḥasan gharīb as per ibn 'Allān, *al-Futūḥāt al-Rabbāniyyah*, vol. 3, pg. 109.

[5] *al-Ra'd* (13): 11

Ibn 'Abbās said, 'They are the angels who guard him by Allāh's command and when the decree comes they withdraw from him.'[6]

'Alī (*raḍiyAllāhu 'anhu*) said, 'Two angels accompany every person guarding him against all that has not been decreed. Then, when the decree comes, they withdraw, leaving him to it. Behold, the appointed time is a fortified shield.'[7]

Mujāhid said, 'There is no servant except that he has an angel safeguarding him against Jinn, man and harmful animals in his moments of sleep and wakefulness. There is nothing that comes to the servant except that he says, "Away with you!" except for something that Allāh has allowed which will then afflict him.'[8]

2.1 Allāh's Safeguarding Health & Wealth

Another example of Allāh's safeguarding His servant is His preserving his health, strength, intellect and wealth. One of the Salaf said, 'The scholar does not become senile.' Another said, 'Whoever memorises the Qur'ān will find his intellect blessed.' Some explained His saying,

ثُمَّ رَدَدْنَٰهُ أَسْفَلَ سَٰفِلِينَ ﴿٥﴾ إِلَّا ٱلَّذِينَ ءَامَنُوا۟ وَعَمِلُوا۟ ٱلصَّٰلِحَٰتِ فَلَهُمْ أَجْرٌ غَيْرُ مَمْنُونٍ ﴿٦﴾

[6] Ṭabarī #20216-20217. Suyūṭī, *al-Durr al-Manthūr*, vol. 4, pg. 614 additionally references it to 'Abdu'l-Razzāq, Faryābī, ibn al-Mundhir and ibn Abī Ḥātim.

[7] Ṭabarī #20247, he said this when he was told that some people had plotted his murder.

[8] Ṭabarī #20245

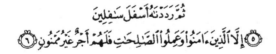

> **"Then We reduced him to the lowest of the low, except for those who have faith and work righteous deeds."**[9]

stating that the *lowest of the low* referred to the decrepitude of old age.[10]

Abū'l-Ṭayyib al-Ṭabarī exceeded the age of one hundred yet his intellect remained very much intact as did his strength. One day he leapt off a large ship he was on onto the ground. When reprimanded for this he said, 'We safeguarded these limbs from sins in our youth, so Allāh has safeguarded them for us in our old age.'[11]

In the opposite vein, Junaid saw an old man begging people and remarked, 'This person was negligent of Allāh in his youth so Allāh has neglected him in his old age.'

Allāh will also safeguard a person, by virtue of his righteousness, through his children and grandchildren. It is said in explanation of His saying,

وَكَانَ أَبُوهُمَا صَـٰلِحًا

[9] *al-Tīn* (95): 5-6

[10] mentioned in **"Allāh created you and then will take you back again. And some of you revert to the lowest form of life so that, after having knowledge, you know nothing at all."** [*al-Naḥl* (16): 70]. cf. *al-Ḥajj* (22): 5

This explanation was given by ibn 'Abbās and recorded by Ṭabari. Suyūṭi, *al-Durr*, additionally references it to ibn Abī Ḥātim and ibn Mardawayh.

[11] Ibn Kathīr, *al-Bidāyah wa'l-Nihāyah*, vol. 12, pg. 80

"Their father was righteous."[12]

that they were safeguarded by virtue of the righteousness of their father.[13]

Muḥammad ibn al-Munkadir said, 'Allāh will safeguard the children and grandchildren of a person by virtue of his righteousness, He will safeguard the city he is in and the settlements surrounding it. They will always be in the protection of Allāh and His cover.'[14]

Ibn al-Musayyab said to his son, 'Son of mine, I increase my prayers because of you in the hope that I will be safeguarded through you, then he recited,

وَكَانَ أَبُوهُمَا صَٰلِحًا

"Their father was righteous."[15]'

'Umar ibn 'Abdu'l-'Azīz said, 'There is no believer who dies except that Allāh will safeguard him though his children and grandchildren.'

---

[12] *al-Kahf* (18): 82

[13] This was stated by ibn 'Abbās and recorded by ibn al-Mubārak, *al-Zuhd* #332 and Ṭabarī.
It was ruled ṣaḥīḥ by Ḥākim #3395 with Dhahabī agreeing.

[14] Abū Nu'aym, *al-Ḥilyah*, vol. 3, pg. 148 and ibn al-Mubārak, *al-Zuhd* #330

[15] *al-Kahf* (18): 82

Yaḥyā ibn Ismā'īl ibn Salamah ibn Kuhayl said, 'I used to have an older sister who became confused, lost her sanity and became unruly. She would stay in a room in the furthest part of our loft and stayed there for ten-odd years. Then at midnight, while we were sleeping, somebody knocked at the door. I said, "Who is there?" She replied, "Kajjah." I said, "My sister?" She replied, "Yes, your sister." I opened the door and she entered the house for the first time in ten years and said, "Someone came to me in a dream and said, 'Allāh has safeguarded your father, Ismā'īl, by virtue of your grandfather, Salamah. He has safeguarded you by virtue of your father so if you wish, supplicate to Allāh and what has afflicted you shall leave you, or you can be patient and Paradise will be yours. Abū Bakr and 'Umar have interceded for you with Allāh, Mighty and Magnificent, through the love your father and grandfather had of them.' So I said, 'If it must be one of the two, I choose patience so that Paradise can be mine. However, Allāh is generous to His creation, nothing is too great for Him, and if He wishes to grant me both, He can.' So it was said to me, 'Allāh has granted you both and is pleased with your father and grandfather because of their love of Abū Bakr and 'Umar. Stand and go down,'" and Allāh relieved her of her affliction.'

When the servant devotes himself to obeying Allāh, Mighty and Magnificent, Allāh will safeguard him in that state as is recorded in the *Musnad* of Imām Aḥmad on the authority of Ḥumayd ibn Hilāl on the authority of someone who said, 'I came to the Prophet (ﷺ) and he showed me a house and said, "A woman used to live here and she went out as part of a Muslim raiding party leaving behind her twelve goats and her weavers hook with which she would weave. She lost a goat from her flock and her hook and so (supplicated), 'My Lord! You have guaranteed the safeguarding of a person who goes out in Your Way. I have lost a goat of mine and my weavers hook. I implore You to return them to me!'" The Messenger of Allāh (ﷺ) commented on the intensity of her imploring her Lord, Blessed and Exalted. He said, "So she awoke in the morning to find her goat and hook with her and the likes of them in addition. If you wish, go and ask her." I said, "I believe you.'"[16]

Shaybān al-Rāʿī would tend to his flocks in the open fields, on the Day of Jumuʿah he would draw a line around them and go and pray the Friday Prayer. He would return to find them in the same place that he had left them.[17]

One of the Salaf would have a balance with which he would weigh dirhams. He heard the call for prayer and so, leaving them scattered on the ground, he went to pray. When he returned, he gathered up the money and nothing of it had been taken.

2.2 Allāh's Safeguarding Against Harm

Another example of Allāh's safeguarding His servant is His preserving him in his worldly life from every Jinn and man who may wish to harm him. He, Most High, says,

وَمَن يَتَّقِ ٱللَّهَ يَجْعَل لَّهُۥ مَخْرَجًا ﴿٢﴾ وَيَرْزُقْهُ مِنْ حَيْثُ لَا يَحْتَسِبُ ۚ

"Whoever has *taqwā* of Allāh - He will give him a way out and provide for him from where he does

[16] Aḥmad #20664
Haythamī, vol. 5, pg. 277 said the narrators were those of the Ṣaḥīḥ.

[17] Abū Nuʿaym, vol. 8, pg. 317

not expect."[18]

'Ā'ishah said, 'He will suffice him from the distress and worry of this world.'[19] Rabī' ibn Khuthaym said, 'He will provide him with a way out from everything that burdens a man.'[20]

'Ā'ishah wrote to Mu'āwiyah, 'If you have *taqwā* of Allāh, He will suffice you in place of people, and if you fear people, they will not be able to avail you in anything against Allāh.'[21]

One of the Khalīfs wrote a letter to Ḥakam ibn 'Amr al-Ghifārī in which he commanded him to do something that opposed the Book of Allāh. In reply, Ḥakam wrote to him saying, 'I looked into the Book of Allāh and saw that it came before the letter of the Leader of the Believers. If the heavens and earth were fused together seamlessly as one unit and a person were to have *taqwā* of Allāh, Mighty and Magnificent, Allāh would give him a way out. Peace.'

One of them composed the following couplets,

By the *taqwā* of Allāh is one rescued
Victory attained and hopes pursued
Whoever has *taqwā*, He will provide
Him a way out; this He did decide.

[18] *al-Ṭalāq* (65): 2

[19] Suyūṭī, *al-Durr* references this to ibn Abī Ḥātim

[20] Ṭabarī

[21] Ibn Abī Shaybah, vol. 14, pg. 61

One of the Salaf wrote to his brother saying, '...to proceed, whoever has *taqwā* of Allāh has safeguarded himself, and whoever neglects the *taqwā* of Allāh has neglected himself and Allāh has absolutely no need of him.'

2.3 Allāh's Safeguarding Against Animals

One of the amazing ways that Allāh safeguards those who safeguard Him is that He makes animals that are normally dangerous guard a person against harm and help him. This is what happened with Safīnah, the freed-slave of the Prophet (ﷺ), when his boat sank and he drifted to an island. There, he saw a lion and said, 'O Abū'l-Ḥārith, I am Safīnah, the freed-slave of the Messenger of Allāh, so the lion walked with him and guided him along the way. Then it purred as if bidding farewell and left.'[22]

Abū Ibrāhīm al-Sā'iḥ fell ill at a place close to a monastery and said, 'If only I were at the door of the monastery, the monks would have come and treated me.' So a lion came and carried him on its back and dropped him by the door of the monastery; the monks, four hundred of them, saw him and accepted Islām.'[23]

Once, Ibrāhīm ibn Adham slept in a garden. By him was a serpent in whose mouth was a circle of daffodils and it remained on guard for him until he awoke.

---

[22] Abū Nu'aym, vol. 1, pg. 369 and Ṭabarānī, *al-Kabir* #6432. It was ruled ṣaḥīḥ by Ḥākim #6550 with Dhahabī agreeing.

[23] Dhahabī, *Siyar*, vol. 11, pp. 228-229 and he said it was munkar.

So whoever safeguards Allāh, Allāh will safeguard him from predatory animals and, moreover, have those animals protect him. Whoever neglects Allāh, Allāh will neglect him to such an extent that he will be harmed by things which he expected benefit from. He may even find the closest members of his family and the most beloved harming him!

One of them said, 'If I disobey Allāh, I see the effects in the mannerisms of my servant and donkey.'[24] He meant that his servant became unruly and disobedient and his donkey refused to carry him.

All good is to be found in obeying Allāh and turning towards Him. All evil is to be found in disobeying Him and turning away from Him.

One of the Gnostics said, 'Whoever leaves the door of his master will never be able to plant his feet firmly on the ground.'

One of them composed the following couplets,

By Allāh, never have I come to visit you
Except that the earth compacted before me.
I have never resolved to leave your door
Except that I tripped over my garment's tail.
For Allāh's sake! Pardon, overlook and mend
My faults for my state with you is as you see.

2. The best and most noble form of preservation: Allāh's safeguarding His servant in his religion.

[24] This was stated by Fuḍayl ibn 'Iyāḍ as in Abū Nu'aym, vol. 8, pg. 109

2.4 Allāh's Safeguarding Against Doubts and Desires

During his lifetime, Allāh preserves the servant's religion and faith by safeguarding him against all vile doubts, misguiding innovations and unlawful desires. Allāh also preserves his religion at the point of his death such that he dies on the religion of Islām.

Ḥakam ibn Abān narrated that Abū Makkī said, 'When death comes to a person it is said to the angel, "Smell his head!" The angel will say, "I smell the fragrance of the Qur'ān." It will be said, "Smell his heart!" The angel will say, "I smell the fragrance of Fasting." It will be said, "Smell his feet!" The angel will say, "I smell the fragrance of the night prayer." He safeguarded his self so Allāh, Mighty and Magnificent, safeguarded him.' It was recorded by ibn Abī al-Dunyā.[25]

The Two Ṣaḥīḥs record on the authority of al-Barā'a ibn 'Āzib that the Prophet (ﷺ) taught him to say, when going to sleep, "O Allāh, if You are to take my soul, bestow mercy on it; and if you are to grant it reprieve, safeguard it with that which You safeguard Your righteous servants."[26]

[25] It is also recorded as a saying of Fuḍayl ibn 'Iyād by Abū Nu'aym, vol. 8, pg. 109

[26] This is the wording of the ḥadīth recorded by Bukhārī #6320-7393 and Muslim #2714 on the authority of Abū Hurayah, The ḥadīth of al-Barā'a is recorded by Bukhārī #6311-6313-7488 and Muslim #2710 with the words, "When you retreat to your bed, perform ablution in the way you would for prayer, then lie down on your right side and say, 'O Allāh, I have submitted my face to you...'"

The ḥadīth of 'Umar mentions that that Prophet (ﷺ) taught him to say, 'O Allāh, safeguard me with Islām when standing, safeguard me with Islām when sitting and safeguard me with Islām when lying down. Answer not the (request) of an envy ridden enemy concerning me.' It was recorded by ibn Ḥibbān in his *Ṣaḥīḥ*.[27]

When the Prophet (ﷺ) would bid a traveller farewell he would say, "I consign your religion, trust and your final assertive deeds to Allāh's care,"[28] another narration mentions that he used to say, "When Allāh consigns something to His care, He safeguards it." This was recorded by Nasā'ī and others.[29]

---

[27] Ibn Ḥibbān #934 with a ḍa'īf isnād.

It has a supporting ḥadīth recorded by Ḥākim #1924 on the authority of ibn Mas'ūd with the words, "O Allāh, safeguard me with Islām when standing, safeguard me with Islām when sitting, safeguard me with Islām when lying down. Do not cause an enemy or envier to rejoice (at a misfortune that befalls me). O Allāh, I ask You for every good, the treasure of which is in Your hand, and I take refuge with You from every evil, the treasure of which is in Your hand."
Suyūṭī, *al-Jāmi' al-Ṣaghīr* #1486 said it was ṣaḥīḥ and Albānī, *al-Ṣaḥīḥah* #1540 ruled it ḥasan due to both ḥadīths supporting each other.

[28] Tirmidhī #3442-3443, Abū Dāwūd #2600, Nasā'ī, *'Amal al-Yawm wa'l-Laylah* #524, ibn Mājah #2826 on the authority of ibn 'Umar.

Tirmidhī said it was ḥasan ṣaḥīḥ gharīb, it was declared ṣaḥīḥ by ibn Ḥibbān #2693 and Ḥākim #2475 with Dhahabī agreeing. Ibn 'Asākir, *Mu'jam al-Shuyūkh*, vol. 2, pg. 780 said it was ḥasan as did ibn Ḥajr as quoted from him by ibn 'Allān, *al-Futūḥāt al-Rabbāniyyah*, vol. 5, pg. 116. Albānī, *al-Ṣaḥīḥah* #14 ruled it ṣaḥīḥ.

The same wording is recorded by Abū Dāwūd #2601 on the authority of 'Abdullāh ibn Yazīd and Nawawī. *Riyāḍ al-Ṣāliḥīn* #294 and *al-Adhkār*, pg. 279 said the isnād was ṣaḥīḥ as did Albānī, *al-Ṣaḥīḥah* #15-1605

[29] Nasā'ī, *'Amal al-Yawm wa'l-Laylah* #506-509-517, ibn Ḥibbān #2376 (*Mawārid*), Bayhaqī, *al-Sunan al-Kabīr*, vol. 9, pg. 173 on the authority of ibn 'Umar with a ḥasan isnād.

Ṭabarānī records a ḥadīth in which the Prophet (ﷺ) said, "When a servant prays the prayer as it should be prayed it rises to Allāh having rays like the rays of the sun and it says to its performer, 'May Allāh preserve you as you have preserved me.' If he was lax and lazy in performing it, it will be wound up like an old garment is wound up and then used to strike the face of its performer while saying, 'May Allāh waste you as you have wasted me!'"[30]

'Umar ibn al-Khaṭṭāb (*raḍiyAllāhu 'anhu*) would say in his sermons, 'O Allāh, protect us with Your preservation and keep us firm on Your command.'

A man once said to one of the Salaf, 'May Allāh preserve you,' to which he replied, 'My brother, do not ask that he be preserved, ask instead that his faith be preserved!' What he meant was to stress the importance of supplicating for the preservation of ones religion; this is because worldly preservation could be conferred on both the righteous and the sinner, but Allāh only safeguards the religion of the believer and comes between it and anything that would pollute it via numerous means, some of which the servant is unaware of and yet others he may dislike.

[30] Ṭabarānī, *al-Awsaṭ* #3095 on the authority of Anas.

'Irāqī, *al-Mughnī* #382 said the isnād was ḍa'īf, he also said that it was recorded by Ṭayālisī on the authority of 'Ubādah ibn al-Ṣāmit with a ḍa'īf isnād. Haythamī, vol. 1, pg. 302, said concerning the ḥadīth of Anas, 'Its isnād contains 'Ubbād ibn Kathīr and his weakness is agreed upon,' and Albānī, *Ḍa'īf al-Targhīb* #221-280 ruled it ḍa'īf jiddan. Concerning the ḥadīth of 'Ubādah, Haythamī, vol. 2, pg. 122 said that it contained the narrator al-Aḥwaṣ ibn Ḥakīm whom ibn al-Madīnī and al-'Ijlī declared thiqah whilst a group declared him ḍa'īf.

This is how He preserved Yūsuf (*'alayhis-salām*) as He said,

كَذَٰلِكَ لِنَصْرِفَ عَنْهُ
ٱلسُّوٓءَ وَٱلْفَحْشَآءَ ۚ إِنَّهُۥ مِنْ عِبَادِنَا ٱلْمُخْلَصِينَ ﴿٢٤﴾

"That happened so that We might avert from him all evil and lust. He was Our chosen servant."[31]

2.5 Allāh's Safeguarding Through Intervention

Whoever is sincere to Allāh, Allāh will safeguard him against evil and indecency, He will guard him against them via means that he is not even aware of, and He will come between him and the routes leading to destructive sin. Ma'rūf al-Karkhī once saw some youths preparing themselves to go for forth for battle at a time of *fitna* and said, 'O Allāh, preserve them!' It was asked of him, 'Why are you supplicating for them?' He replied, 'If He were to preserve them, they would not leave to carry out what they intend.'

'Umar heard a person saying, 'O Allāh, you intervene between a person and his heart, so intervene between me and my disobeying You.' This pleased 'Umar and he supplicated for that person.

In exegesis to the saying of Allāh, Most High,

فَٱعْلَمُوٓا۟ أَنَّ ٱللَّهَ مَوْلَىٰكُمْ ۚ نِعْمَ ٱلْمَوْلَىٰ وَنِعْمَ ٱلنَّصِيرُ

[31] *Yūsuf* (12): 24

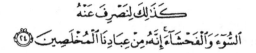

"Know that Allāh intervenes between a man and his heart."[32]

Ibn 'Abbās said, 'He intervenes between the believer and (his committing) sins that would drag him into the Fire.'[33]

One of the previous people performed Ḥajj; while sleeping at Mecca with a group of people, he had the sudden urge to commit a sin and heard a voice crying out, 'Woe to you! Are you not performing Ḥajj?!' Hence Allāh guarded him against perpetrating the sin.

One person went out with a group of people desiring to commit a particular sin, when he was about to do it, a voice cried out,

كُلُّ نَفْسٍ بِمَا كَسَبَتْ رَهِينَةٌ ﴿٣٨﴾

"Every self is held in pledge against what it has earned,"[34]

and so he abandoned it.

A man entered a thicket dense with trees and said, 'I could commit my sin here in secret, who is there to see me?' He then heard a voice reverberating throughout the thicket (reciting the verse),

---

[32] *al-Anfāl* (8): 24

[33] Ṭabarī #15880-15881.
It was ruled ṣaḥīḥ by Ḥākim #3265 with Dhahabī agreeing.

[34] *al-Muddaththir* (74): 38

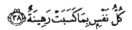

أَلَا يَعْلَمُ مَنْ خَلَقَ وَهُوَ اللَّطِيفُ الْخَبِيرُ ﴿١٤﴾

"Does He who created not then know? He is the All-Pervading, the All-Aware."[35]

Another desired to commit a sin and left to carry it out. While walking, he passed by a story-teller plying his trade amongst the people. He stood there listening and heard him saying, 'O you who desire to commit a sin! Do you not know that the Creator of desires is fully aware of your intent?' At this he fell in a swoon and, when he regained consciousness, immediately repented.

One of the righteous kings had fallen in love with a beautiful subject of his. He feared for himself and so stood in prayer by night, seeking succour from Allāh. That same night, the subject fell ill and passed away three days later.

2.6 Allāh's Safeguarding Through Exhortation

Some people were safeguarded through an exhortation given by someone they wanted to be an accomplice in sin. An example of this lies with one of the three who entered the cave that was subsequently blocked by a boulder. (The ḥadīth) mentions that one of them, when he lay with the woman ready to perform intercourse she said, 'Fear Allāh and do not break the seal except by due right,' so he left her.[36]

---

[35] *al-Mulk* (67): 14

[36] Bukhārī #2215-2272-2333-3465-5974 and Muslim #2743 on the authority of ibn 'Umar

Another example lies with the story of Kifl, a man of the Children of Israel who committed sin frequently. He was attracted to a woman and gave her sixty dīnārs and then lay with her ready to perform intercourse. She began trembling with fear and so he asked her, 'Am I forcing you?' She replied, 'No, but I have never done such a thing before and it was only need that has forced me.' He said, 'You are fearful of Allāh, should I not fear Him as well?' Then he stood and left her, leaving her the money as a gift. He then said, 'By Allāh, Kifl will never disobey Allāh again.' He passed away that same night and the following morning saw these words inscribed on his door, 'Allāh has forgiven Kifl.' This was recorded by Imām Aḥmad and Tirmidhī on the authority of ibn 'Umar to the Messenger (ﷺ).[37]

A man sought to seduce a woman and ordered her to lock the doors, which she did. She then said, 'One door remains open.' He asked, 'What door would that be?' She replied, 'The door between Allāh, Mighty and Magnificent, and us.' So he turned away from her.

Another sought to seduce a desert Arab. He said, 'Who is there to see us save the stars?' 'What of the One who put them there?' she replied.[38]

All of these are examples of Allāh's providence and His intervening between the servant and his committing sin. While men-

---

[37] Aḥmad #4747 and Tirmidhī #2496
Tirmidhī said it was ḥasan but ibn Kathīr, *al-Bidāyah wa'l-Nihāyah*, vol. 1, pg. 226, said, 'It is a very odd ḥadīth and its isnād is problematic.' Albānī, *al-Ḍa'īfah* #4083 ruled it ḍa'īf and Arna'ūṭ et. al. ruled the isnād ḍa'īf.

[38] cf. ibn al-Jawzī, *Dhamm al-Hawā'*, pg. 272

tioning the sinners, al-Ḥasan said, 'Their worth was diminished with Him, so they disobeyed Him. Were they to have held a position of worth and honour with Him, He would have preserved them.' Bishr said, 'One who is noble or honoured would never persist in disobeying Allāh and neither would the sagacious give preference to this world over the Hereafter.'

2.7 Allāh's Ensuring the Best for His Servant

Another example of Allāh's preserving the religion of His servant is that a servant could pursue a worldly office such as leadership or undertake a worldly enterprise such as trade and Allāh, knowing what is good for him, intervenes between him and his goal. The servant, heedless of what has taken place, hates what has happened.

Ibn Mas'ūd said, 'A servant intends to undertake a trading venture or aims for leadership hoping that it will be facilitated for him. Allāh will look at him and say to the Angels, "Avert him from it for if I was to make this matter easy for him, I would cause him to enter the Fire!" So Allāh would avert him from it and he, in a state of agitation, will complain, "So-and-so beat me! So-and-so outsmarted me!" Yet all it is, is Allāh's good-grace, Mighty and Magnificent is He!'

Yet more astonishing is that a servant could strive to do an action of obedience, however this particular action would not be the best course for him, so Allāh will intervene between him and it in order to preserve him, and he, all the while, remains heedless.

Ṭabarānī and others records the ḥadīth of Anas that the Messenger of Allāh (ﷺ) said, "Allāh, Mighty and Magnificent, says, 'Amongst My servants are those whose faith can only be made good through poverty, and were I to give him freely, his faith would be sullied. Amongst My servants are those whose faith can only be made good through affluence, and were I to make him poor, his faith would be sullied. Amongst My servants are those whose faith can only be made good through sound health, and were I to make him ill, his faith would be sullied. Amongst My servants are those whose faith can only be made good through illness, and were I to make him healthy his faith would be sullied. Amongst My servants are those who seek to do an act of worship but I prevent him from doing it lest he fall prey to conceit. I regulate the affairs of My servants in accordance to My knowledge of what is in their hearts. I am the All-Knowing, the All-Aware.'"[39]

One of the early people would frequently ask for martyrdom, so a voice called out, 'If you were to embark on a military expedition, you would be captured and during your captivity you would convert to Christianity, so stop asking for this.'

Therefore, in summary, whoever safeguards the limits of Allāh and carefully tends to His rights, Allāh will undertake to safeguard him in his worldly and religious life, in this world and the next.

---

[39] Ibn Abī al-Dunyā, *al-Awliyā'*, pg. 100, Abū Nu'aym, vol. 8, pg. 318, Bayhaqī, *al-Asmā' wa'l-Ṣifāt*, pg. 150.

Abū Nu'aym said that the ḥadīth was gharīb and ibn Rajab, *Jamī' al-'Ulūm*, vol. 2, pg. 333 said, 'It contains al-Khushanī and Ṣadaqah both of whom are ḍa'īf, and Hishām who is not known.' Albānī, *al-Ḍa'īfah* #1775 ruled it ḍa'īf jiddan.

2.8 Allāh is the Protector of the Believers

In His Book, Allāh, Most High, has informed us that He is the Protector of the believers and that He protects the righteous; subsumed by this is the fact that He safeguards what is good for them in both this life and the Hereafter, and that He will not abandon them to another. Allāh, Most High, says,

ٱللَّهُ وَلِيُّ ٱلَّذِينَ ءَامَنُوا۟ يُخْرِجُهُم مِّنَ ٱلظُّلُمَٰتِ إِلَى ٱلنُّورِ

"Allāh is the Protector of those who have faith; He brings them out of the darkness into the light."[40]

ذَٰلِكَ بِأَنَّ ٱللَّهَ مَوْلَى ٱلَّذِينَ ءَامَنُوا۟ وَأَنَّ ٱلْكَٰفِرِينَ لَا مَوْلَىٰ لَهُمْ ﴿١١﴾

"That is because Allāh is the Protector of those who have faith and because the disbelievers have no protector."[41]

وَمَن يَتَوَكَّلْ عَلَى ٱللَّهِ فَهُوَ حَسْبُهُۥٓ

"Whoever puts his trust in Allāh, He will be enough for him."[42]

أَلَيْسَ ٱللَّهُ بِكَافٍ عَبْدَهُۥ

[40] *al-Baqarah* (2): 257

[41] *Muḥammad* (47): 11

[42] *al-Ṭalāq* (65): 3

"Is Allāh not enough for His slave?"[43]

Whoever establishes the rights of Allāh, Allāh will undertake to upkeep everything that will be of benefit to him in this life and the next. Whoever wants Allāh to preserve him and tend to all of his affairs, let him first tend to the rights of Allāh upon him. Whoever does not wish to be afflicted by anything he dislikes, let him not undertake that which Allāh dislikes.

One of the Salaf would go to gathering after gathering saying, 'Whoever wants Allāh to preserve his well-being, let him have *taqwā* of Allāh.'

al-'Umarī, the ascetic, would say to anyone who asked him for advice, 'Be with Allāh, Mighty and Magnificent, in exactly the same way that you want Him to be with you.'

Ṣāliḥ ibn 'Abdu'l-Karīm said, 'Allāh, Mighty and Magnificent, says, "By My Might and Magnificence, I do not look at a heart that I know predominately loves to adhere resolutely to My obedience except that I undertake to protect his circumstances and keep him firm."'

One of the earlier scriptures mentions, 'Allāh, Mighty and Magnificent, says, "Son of Ādam, will you not tell me what gives you cause to laugh? Son of Ādam, have *taqwā* of Me and then sleep wherever you wish!"'

What this means is that when you establish what is due to Allāh

[43] *al-Zumar* (39): 36

of *taqwā* then do not worry any more about those things that will be good for you, for Allāh knows them better than you and He will direct them to you in the best of ways.

The ḥadīth of Jābir has the Prophet (ﷺ) saying, "Whoever wants to know the standing he has with Allāh, let him look to himself and see the standing that Allāh has with him. Allāh grants a person the same standing as Allah has with that person."[44]

This proves that Allāh's concern with His servant and His safeguarding him is commensurate to the servant's concern with the rights of Allāh, establishing them, tending to His limits and safeguarding them. Whoever's goal is Allāh's good-pleasure, seeking to draw close to Him, knowing Him, loving Him, and serving Him, will find that Allāh will treat him accordantly. Allāh, Most High, says,

فَٱذْكُرُونِىٓ أَذْكُرْكُمْ

"Remember Me, I will remember you."[45]

وَأَوْفُوا۟ بِعَهْدِىٓ أُوفِ بِعَهْدِكُمْ

"Honour My contract and I will honour your

[44] Abū Ya'lā #1865-2138, Ṭabarānī, *al-Awsaṭ* #2501.
Ḥākim #1820 said it was ṣaḥīḥ but Dhahabī said, 'It contains 'Umar who is ḍa'īf.' Haythamī, vol. 10, pg. 77 said, 'Its isnād contains 'Umar ibn 'Abdullāh, the freed slave of Ghufrah, who was declared thiqah by more than one scholar and ḍa'īf by a group of scholars, the remaining narrators are those of the Ṣaḥīḥ.' Albānī, *al-Ḍa'īfah* #5427-6205 ruled it ḍa'īf.

[45] *al-Baqarah* (2): 152

contract."[46]

Moreover, Allāh is the kindest of the kind. He rewards a good deed tenfold and more. Whoever comes close to Him by a hand-span, He comes close to him by a cubit, whoever comes close to Him by a cubit, He comes close to him by a fathom, and whoever comes to Him walking, He comes to him running.[47]

Whatever a person is given is from his self, and nothing afflicts him that he dislikes except that it is as a result of his falling short in fulfilling the rights of his Lord. 'Alī (*raḍiyAllāhu 'anhu*) said, 'The servant must place his hope in his Lord and his Lord alone, and he has nothing to fear save his sins.'

One of them said, 'Whoever clarifies and purifies will be purified, and whoever mixes will be treated accordingly.'

Masrūq said, 'Whoever diligently observes Allāh with respect to the notions and whims of his heart, Allāh will safeguard the motions of his limbs for him.'

There is much more that can be said about this but what we have mentioned thus far suffices and all praise is due to Allāh.

---

[46] *al-Baqarah* (2): 40

[47] As mentioned in a ḥadīth recorded by Bukhārī #7405 and Muslim #2687-2743 on the authority of Abū Hurayrah with the words, "Whoever draws close to me by a hand-span length I draw closer to him by a cubit. Whoever draws closer to me by a cubit, I draw closer to him by a fathom. Whoever comes to Me walking, I go to Him running." The narration of Aḥmad #21374 on the authority of Abū Dharr adds, "And Allāh is more exalted and greater, Allāh is more exalted and greater." Haythamī, vol. 10, p. 197, said the isnād was ḥasan.

CHAPTER THREE

Allāh is With You

The Messenger of Allāh (ﷺ) said, "Safeguard Allāh and you will find Him in front of you," another narration mentions, "Safeguard Allāh and you will find Him before you." The meaning is that whoever safeguards the limits of Allāh and carefully tends to His rights will find Allāh with him in all affairs, encompassing him, aiding him, preserving him, supporting him, setting his foot firm and granting him divine accord. He is *"standing over every self seeing everything that it does,"*[1] and He, Most High, *"is with those who have* taqwā *of Him and with those who do good."*[2]

Qatādah said, 'Allāh is with those who have *taqwā* of Him. Whoever has Allāh with him, then with him is the party that will never be overcome, the sentry that will never sleep and the guide who will never go astray.'[3]

One of the Salaf wrote to one of his brothers saying, 'As for

---

[1] *al-Ra'd* (13): 33

[2] *al-Naḥl* (16): 128

[3] Abū Nu'aym, vol. 2, pg. 340

what follows...If Allāh is with you then who do you have to fear? If He is against you then who can you hope in? Peace!'

This 'withness' is the specific and special type which is reserved for those who have *taqwā*. It is not the general 'withness' that is mentioned in His saying,

وَهُوَ مَعَكُمْ أَيْنَ مَا كُنتُمْ

"He is with you wherever you are."[4]

وَلَا يَسْتَخْفُونَ مِنَ ٱللَّهِ وَهُوَ مَعَهُمْ إِذْ يُبَيِّتُونَ مَا لَا يَرْضَىٰ مِنَ ٱلْقَوْلِ

"...but they cannot conceal themselves from Allāh. He is with them when they spend the night saying things which are not pleasing to Him."[5]

The specific 'withness' dictates aid, support and preservation as Allāh said to Mūsā and Hārūn,

إِنَّنِي مَعَكُمَآ أَسْمَعُ وَأَرَىٰ

"I am with you, All-Hearing and All-Seeing."[6]

He, Most High, says,

[4] *al-Ḥadīd* (57): 4

[5] *al-Nisā'* (4): 108

[6] *Ṭā Hā* (20): 46

ing in its specific sense is what is referred to in the ḥadīth, "the servant continues coming close to Me through performing optional deeds until I love him. When I love him, I become his hearing by which he hears, his seeing with which he sees, his hand with which he strikes, and his foot with which he walks."[11]

There are many texts of the Book and Sunnah that prove that the Lord, Glorious is He, is close to those who obey Him and have *taqwā* of Him, who safeguard His limits and carefully tend to His (rights).

While on the way to Tabūk, Bunān al-Ḥammāl entered an open land and suddenly felt alone; a voice cried out, 'Why do you feel alone? Is not your Beloved with you?'[12]

Therefore, whoever safeguards Allāh and carefully tends to His rights, he will find Him in front of him and before him in every

---

[11] Bukhārī #6502 on the authority of Abū Hurayrah

Similar aḥādīth have also been reported on the authority of 'Ā'ishah by Aḥmad; Abū Umāmah by Ṭabarānī; 'Alī by Ismā'īlī, *Musnad 'Alī*; Ibn 'Abbās by Ṭabarānī; Anas by Ṭabarānī; and Maymūnah by Abū Ya'lā.

Ibn Rajab, *Taḥqīq Kalimatu'l-Ikhlāṣ*, said, 'The meaning is that when love fills the heart and overcomes it, the limbs will then do only that which is pleasing to the Lord. At this point the soul will find tranquillity and peace for it will have been obliterated such that it follows the desire of its Lord as opposed to its own desires.

Servant of Allāh, worship Him as He desires of you, not as you would desire of Him. Whoever worships Allāh in this latter way is worshipping Him as if on a crumbling precipice: if good comes his way, he is happy; but if trial comes his way, he turns on his heel and loses out both in this world and the Hereafter. When gnosis and love become strong, the person will desire only that which his Master desires.'

[12] Abū Nu'aym, vol. 10, pg. 324

circumstance. He will take comfort with Him and suffice with Him in lieu of His creation. The ḥadīth mentions, "The best (quality) of faith is that the servant knows that Allāh is with him wherever he be." This was recorded by Ṭabarānī and others.[13]

To explain this point fully will cause the discussion to become very lengthy.[14]

One of the sagacious scholars was given to travelling alone, once some people came to bid him farewell and he replied by reciting the following couplet,

When we embark by night with You before us
Your mention is sufficient provision to guide us

Shiblī would repeat these couplets and would sometimes end his gathering with them.

---

[13] Ṭabarānī, *al-Kabir* and *al-Awsaṭ* #8796, Abū Nu'aym, vol. 6, pg. 124 on the authority of 'Ubādah ibn al-Ṣamit.

It was declared ḍa'īf by Suyūṭi, *al-Jāmi' al-Ṣaghīr* #1243 and Albānī, *al-Ḍa'īfah* #2589.

[14] Ibn Rajab, *Kashf al-Kurbah*, writes, 'Many of them would not have the strength to interact with the creation and, as a result, would flee so that they could be alone with their beloved; this is why many of them would spend long periods of time in seclusion. When one of them was asked, 'Do you not feel the bite of loneliness?' He replied, 'How can I when He has said that He is the companion of one who remembers Him?' Another said, 'How can one feel the bite of loneliness when he is with Allāh?' Yet another said, 'Whoever feels the bite of loneliness when alone does so because of his lack of solace with his Lord.'

Yaḥyā ibn Mu'ādh would frequently seclude and isolate himself, when his brother censured him for this by saying, 'If you are a man amongst men, you need the company of men,' he replied, 'If you are a man amongst men, you are in need

=

=

of Allāh.' It was once asked of him, 'You have migrated from the people, with whom do you live?' He replied, 'With the One for whose sake I migrated.' Ghazwān was once censured for his seclusion to which he said, 'I attain relief in my heart by sitting with One who meets my needs.'

Because they are regarded to be strange, it is possible that some of them be accused of insanity just as Owais was accused. Abū Muslim al-Khawlānī would frequently perform *dhikr*, his tongue would always move in the remembrance of Allāh and so a man asked one of his companions, 'Is your friend mad?' Abū Muslim replied, 'My brother, no, rather this is the cure for madness!' al-Ḥasan said, while describing them, 'When the ignoramus looks at them, he thinks them ill, yet far are they from illness! He would say they have lost their minds, indeed they have lost their minds to a great matter, far loftier than their accusations, by Allāh they are busied with it from your worldly lot!' It is in this regard that the poet said,

By love's sanctity! I find none to replace You,
O Master! I have no objective save You.
Talking about You makes them say, 'He has a malady!'
I say, 'May that malady never leave me!"

CHAPTER FOUR

Knowing Allāh

The Messenger of Allāh (ﷺ) said, "Know Allāh in times of ease and He will know you in times of hardship," the meaning is that the servant, when he has *taqwā* of Allāh, preserves His limits, and carefully tends to His rights in times of ease and well-being has come to know Allāh. This gives rise to a gnosis between himself and Allāh and, as a result, his Lord will know him in times of hardship: He will know the deeds he worked during times of ease and by virtue of that knowledge will relieve him of hardship.

This too is a specific gnosis which leads to the closeness of Allāh, Mighty and Magnificent, His loving His servant and His responding to his supplication. What is not meant is a general gnosis for nothing of His creation is hidden from Allāh. Allāh, Most High, says,

هُوَ أَعْلَمُ بِكُمْ
إِذْ أَنشَأَكُم مِّنَ ٱلْأَرْضِ وَإِذْ أَنتُمْ أَجِنَّةٌ فِى بُطُونِ أُمَّهَٰتِكُمْ

"He has most knowledge of you when He first produced you from the earth and when you were

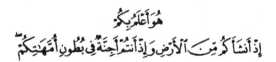

embryos in your mothers' wombs."[1]

وَلَقَدْ خَلَقْنَا ٱلْإِنسَٰنَ وَنَعْلَمُ مَا تُوَسْوِسُ بِهِۦ نَفْسُهُۥ

"We created man and We know what his own self whispers to him."[2]

This specific knowing is alluded to in the ḥadīth qudsī, "...my servant continues to draw closer to Me by performing the optional deeds until I love him. When I love him, I am his hearing by which he hears, his sight by which he sees, his hand with which he strikes, and his leg with which he walks. Were he to ask of Me, I would grant him, and were he to take refuge with Me, I would grant him refuge."[3]

Fuḍayl met Sha'wānah, the worshipper, and asked her to supplicate for him. She said, 'What bars you from Him? If you invoke Him, He will answer you,' upon which he swooned and fell unconscious.[4]

Abū Ja'far al-Sā'iḥ said that al-Ḥasan came to Ḥabīb, Abū Muḥammad, on the run from Ḥajjāj. He said, 'Abū Muḥammad! Hide me from the police; they are hot on my tracks!' He replied, 'Abū Sa'īd, I am ashamed of you! Is there not a (relationship) of

[1] *al-Najm* (53): 32

[2] *Qāf* (50): 16

[3] Bukhārī #6502 on the authority of Abū Hurayrah.

[4] Abū Nu'aym, vol. 8, p. 116 #11567, the narrative continues to quote Fuḍayl as saying, 'Ennoble us with the nobility of obedience and do not humiliate us with the humiliation of disobedience.'

trust between you and your Lord so that you could invoke Him and have Him conceal you from these? Enter the house.' The police entered after him but they did not see him. This was mentioned to Ḥajjāj and he commented, 'Rather, he was in the house but Allāh obscured their sight so they could not see him.'

When this specific knowledge comes about, a special gnosis is engendered between the servant and his Lord that effectuates a sense of comfort and intimacy with Him coupled with a sense of shyness to Him. This special gnosis is not the same as the general gnosis that exists for all believers, and it is to this gnosis that the Gnostics aspire and their words allude to.

Abū Sulaymān heard a man saying, 'I spent last night talking about women.' He said, 'Woe to you! Have you no shame before Him? He sees you spending the night mentioning something besides Him! But how can you be bashful before One you do not even know!'

Aḥmad ibn 'Āṣim al-Anṭākī said, 'My wish is to die after knowing my Master. Knowing Him does not mean affirming (His existence), rather it is that knowledge which, if you know, leads you to being shy of Him.'

This special gnosis and specific knowledge leads the servant to be content with his Lord, to rely on Him and trust Him to deliver him from every hardship and distress, just as it leads to the Lord responding to his supplication.

When al-Ḥasan al-Baṣrī hid from Ḥajjāj it was suggested to him to flee to Baṣrah for fear of his being discovered. He wept and said, 'I should leave my town, family and brothers?! My knowledge of my Lord and His blessings which He has graced me with leads me to believe that He will save me and deliver me from him, if Allāh, Most High, so wills.' Ḥajjāj never harmed him at all, instead, after this, he would greatly honour him and speak well of him.

It was asked of Ma'rūf, 'What is it that has roused in you the desire for seclusion and worship?' The questioner mentioned death, the *barzakh*, and Paradise and Hell as possible causes to which he replied, 'What is this! All of this is in His hand, when there exists a gnosis between you and Him, He suffices you during all of this.'

The ḥadīth recorded by Tirmidhī on the authority of Abū Hurayrah further clarifies this: the Prophet (ﷺ) said, "Whoever wants Allāh to answer him at times of hardship should frequently invoke him in times of ease."[5]

Ibn Abī al-Dunyā, ibn Abī Hātim, ibn Jarīr and others record the ḥadīth of Yazīd al-Raqāshī, on the authority of Anas that the Prophet (ﷺ) said, "While in the belly of the whale, when Yūnus (*'alayhis-salām*) was supplicating, the Angels said, 'This is a familiar voice, yet coming from a strange land!' Allāh said, 'Do you not know who this is?' They asked, 'Who is it?' He replied, 'My servant, Yūnus.' They said, 'Yūnus, Your servant, the one whose deeds have always been accepted and whose supplication has always been answered?' He said, 'Yes.' They said, 'Lord! Will you

---

[5] Tirmidhī #3382 who said it was gharīb.

It was ruled ṣaḥīḥ by Ḥākim #1997 and Dhahabī agreed. Mundhirī, *al-Targhib*, vol. 2, pg. 388 said that its isnād was ṣaḥīḥ or ḥasan. It was declared ḥasan by Suyūṭī, *al-Jāmi' al-Ṣaghīr* #8743 and Albānī, *al-Ṣaḥīḥah* #593, *Ṣaḥīḥ al-Targhib* #1628

not show mercy on him in this time of adversity by virtue of what he used to do in times of ease?' He replied, 'Of course,' and ordered the whale to cast him out on the desert shore."[6]

Ḍaḥḥāk ibn Qays said, 'Remember Allāh in times of ease and He will remember you in times of adversity. Yūnus (*'alayhis-salām*) would remember Allāh, then when he was swallowed by the whale, Allāh, Most High, said,

فَلَوْلَآ أَنَّهُۥ
كَانَ مِنَ ٱلْمُسَبِّحِينَ ﴿١٤٣﴾ لَلَبِثَ فِى بَطْنِهِۦٓ إِلَىٰ يَوْمِ يُبْعَثُونَ ﴿١٤٤﴾

"Had it not been that he was a man who glorified Allāh, he would have remained inside its belly until the Day they are raised again."[7]

Pharaoh was an oppressor, heedless of the remembrance of Allāh. When he was drowning, he said, "I believe!" and Allāh, Most High, said,

ءَآلْـَٔـٰنَ وَقَدْ عَصَيْتَ قَبْلُ وَكُنتَ مِنَ ٱلْمُفْسِدِينَ ﴿٩١﴾

"What, now! When previously you rebelled and were one of the corrupters?"[8]'

Rishdīn ibn Sa'd said, 'A man asked Abū'l-Dardā' to advise him.

[6] Ibn Abī al-Dunyā, *al-Faraj ba'd al-Shidda*, pg. 25 with a ḍa'īf isnād

[7] *al-Ṣāffāt* (37): 143-144

[8] *Yūnus* (10): 91

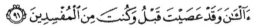

He replied, "Remember Allāh in times of ease and He will remember you in times of hardship.'"[9]

Salmān al-Fārisī said, 'If a man is given to supplicating in times of ease and is then faced with hardship, and supplicates to Allāh, Mighty and Magnificent, the Angels say, "This is a familiar voice...," and intercede for him. If he is not given to supplicating in times of ease and is then faced with hardship and supplicates to Allāh, Mighty and Magnificent, the Angels will say, "This is an unfamiliar voice," and they will not intercede for him.'

The ḥadīth about the three people who entered a cave only to be blocked in by a falling boulder also lends weight to this; they were saved because they invoked Allāh, adducing righteous deeds they had previously performed while in a state of ease: being dutiful to parents, leaving a lewd act, and fulfilling a trust that would not have been known to people at large.[10]

It is now known that knowing Allāh in times of ease leads to Allāh's knowing His servant in times of hardship. It is also known that there is no hardship that the believer will face in this world worse than death; this hardship is actually lighter than what follows if the destination of the servant is not good, or it is the worst he will face if his destination is good. As such, it becomes obligatory for the servant to prepare for death before it sets on him by performing righteous deeds and hastening to do so. A person does not know in which day or night he will be beset by

[9] Abū Nu'aym, vol. 1, pg. 209

[10] Bukhārī #2215-2272-2333-3465-5974 and Muslim #2743 on the authority of ibn 'Umar

this hardship.

Remembering righteous deeds at the time of death vivifies one's good opinion of his Lord, helps alleviate the throes of death and strengthen one's hope.

One of them said, 'They would consider it recommended for a person to have a cache of righteous deeds that would serve to alleviate the onset of death,' or words to that effect.

They would also consider it praiseworthy for a person to die after having completed an action of worship such as pilgrimage, or jihād or fasting.

Nakha'ī said, 'They would consider it praiseworthy to remind a servant on his deathbed of his good works so that he could make good his opinion of his Lord.'

While sick, Abū Abdu'l-Raḥmān al-Sulamī said, 'How can I not have hope in my Lord seeing that I have fasted for his sake for eighty Ramaḍans?'[11]

When death came to Abū Bakr ibn 'Ayyāsh and those around him wept, he said, 'Do not cry, for I have finished the Qur'ān in this place of prayer thirteen thousand times!'

It is reported that he said to his son, 'Do you think that Allāh would waste forty years of your fathers life every night of which he completed the Qur'ān?'[12]

[11] Abū Nu'aym, vol. 4, pg. 192

[12] Khaṭīb, *Tārīkh*, vol. 14, pg. 383

While on his deathbed, one of the Salaf saw his son crying and said, 'Do not cry for your father has never committed an indecent act.'

Ādam ibn Abū Iyās finished the Qur'ān while he was already shrouded, waiting for his death. He exclaimed, 'By my love of You! Be gentle to me at this terrible time. My hopes and expectation were in You all this time in preparation for this day. There is none worthy of worship save Allāh!' and upon saying this, he passed away, may Allāh have mercy on him.[13]

On his deathbed, 'Abdu'l-Ṣamad, the ascetic, said, 'My Master, it is for this time that I have kept You as my hidden store, it is for this day that I have secured You, give reality to my good opinion of You!'[14]

At the time of his death, the women around him weeping, ibn 'Aqīl said, 'I have been sealing verdicts for Him for fifty years, leave me alone to prepare for meeting Him. '

When the Qarāmiṭah attacked the pilgrims, slaughtering them while they were performing *ṭawāf*, 'Alī ibn Bākwayh, the Ṣūfī, was also performing it, yet he did not stop his *ṭawāf* despite being struck repeatedly by swords, until at last he fell. He was reciting the following couplets,

> You see the lovers lying
> in their homes prostrate,

[13] Khaṭīb, *Tārīkh*, vol. 7, pg. 29

[14] Ibn al-Jawzī, *Ṣifatu'l-Ṣafwah*, vol. 2, pg. 272

Like the people of the cave,
unaware of how long they tarried.
By Allāh! Were the lovers to swear
that on the day of conflict
They are like those already dead,
they would not be untruthful.

Whoever, during his life, obeys Allāh and safeguards His limits, Allāh will take care of him on his deathbed and allow him to die on faith. He will make him firm with the firm word in his grave when questioned by the two angels and repress the punishment of the grave from him, and He will give solace to his loneliness at that time of isolation and in that darkness.

One of the Salaf said, 'If Allāh is with you when you enter the grave, you will not be harmed nor will you be lonely.'

After his death, one of the righteous scholars was seen in a dream and was asked after his condition. He replied, 'My Lord, Mighty and Magnificent, keeps me company.'

Whoever, in this world, has Allāh as his companion in times of retreat and being alone, he can truly hope that Allāh will be his companion in the darkness of the grave's niche when he leaves this world. It is in this sense that one of them said,

When I feel isolated, lonely
My Lord! Be my companion.
For I have believed completely
in Your revelation.
That to Allāh I do journey,
leaves me with no trepidation.

More than my family,
He shows kindness, compassion!

The same applies to the terror of the Day of Rising, its horrors and hardships: when Allāh takes care of his obedient servant, He will deliver him from all of this.

Qatādah said in explanation to His, Most High's, saying,

وَمَن يَتَّقِ ٱللَّهَ يَجۡعَل لَّهُۥ مَخۡرَجٗا ﴿٢﴾

"Whoever has *taqwā* of Allāh - He will give him a way out."[15]

'(He will give him a way out) from the hardship of death and the terrors of the Day of Rising.'[16]

'Alī ibn Abū Ṭalḥah narrated that ibn 'Abbās (*raḍiyAllāhu 'anhumā*) said in commentary to this verse, 'We will deliver him from every hardship in this world and the Hereafter.'[17]

Concerning the saying of Allāh, Most High,

---

[15] *al-Ṭalāq* (65): 2

[16] Suyūṭī, *al-Durr al-Manthūr*, vol. 14, pg. 537 references this to 'Abd ibn Ḥumayd and Abū Nu'aym, *al-Ḥilyah* (vol. 2, pg. 340)

[17] Ṭabarī, vol. 23, pg. 43. Suyūṭī, *al-Durr al-Manthūr*, vol. 14, pg. 538 references this to ibn al-Mundhir and ibn Abī Ḥātim

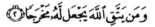

إِنَّ ٱلَّذِينَ قَالُوا۟ رَبُّنَا ٱللَّهُ ثُمَّ ٱسْتَقَٰمُوا۟ تَتَنَزَّلُ عَلَيْهِمُ
ٱلْمَلَٰٓئِكَةُ أَلَّا تَخَافُوا۟ وَلَا تَحْزَنُوا۟ وَأَبْشِرُوا۟ بِٱلْجَنَّةِ
ٱلَّتِى كُنتُمْ تُوعَدُونَ ﴿٣٠﴾

"Those who say, 'Our Lord is Allāh,' and then go straight, the angels descend on them: 'Do not fear and do not grieve but rejoice in the Garden you have been promised.'"[18]

Zayd ibn Aslam said, 'He will be given glad-tidings at the point of his death, in his grave and the Day he is resurrected. He will find himself in Paradise before the joy of the good news has a chance to leave his heart!'[19]

Thābit al-Bunānī said in commentary to this verse, 'It has reached us that the two angels who accompanied him in this world will meet the believer when Allāh resurrects him from his grave. They will say, *"Do not fear, do not grieve,"* and Allāh will alleviate his fear and give comfort to his eye. There is not a single terror that will overcome man on the Day of Rising except that it will be a source of comfort for the believer because Allāh has guided him and because of what he worked in this life.'[20] All of these were recorded by ibn Abī Ḥātim and others.

---

[18] Fuṣṣilat (41): 30, cf. *al-Aḥqāf* (46): 13

[19] Suyūṭī, *al-Durr al-Manthūr*, vol. 13, pg. 107 references this to ibn Abī Shaybah and ibn Abī Ḥātim

[20] Suyūṭī, *al-Durr al-Manthūr*, vol. 13, pg. 108 references this to ibn al-Mundhir and ibn Abī Ḥātim

As regards one who does not know Allāh in times of ease, he will have no one to know him in times of adversity, not in this life or in the Hereafter! Seeing the condition of such a person in this world testifies to this fact and their condition in the Hereafter will be even worse for they will have no protector or helper.

CHAPTER FIVE

Asking Allāh

The Messenger of Allāh (ﷺ) said, "When you ask, ask Allāh." Allāh, Mighty and Magnificent, commanded that He Alone be asked and prohibited asking another. Allāh, Most High, has ordered that He be asked,

وَسْـَٔلُوا۟ ٱللَّهَ مِن فَضْلِهِۦٓ

"...ask Allāh for His bounty."[1]

Tirmidhī records the ḥadīth of ibn Mas'ūd that the Messenger of Allāh (ﷺ) said, "Ask Allāh for His bounty for Allāh loves to be asked."[2]

---

[1] *al-Nisā'* (4): 32

[2] Tirmidhī #3571, Ṭabarānī, *al-Kabir*, vol. 10, pg. 124.
'Ijlūnī, *Kashf al-Khafā'* #1507 said that it was declared ḍa'īf by 'Irāqī and ḥasan by ibn Ḥajr. It was declared ḍa'īf by Albānī, *al-Ḍa'īfah* #492. 'Irāqī, *al-Mughnī* #987 said that its isnād contains Ḥammād ibn Wāqid who ibn Ma'īn and others declared ḍa'īf. Sakhāwī, *Maqāṣid al-Ḥasanah* #195 quotes Bayhaqī as saying, 'Ḥammād was alone in reporting it and he is not strong.'

He also records the ḥadīth of Abū Hurayrah that the Prophet (ﷺ) said, "Allāh is angry at whoever does not ask of Him."[3]

He also records the ḥadīth, "Allāh loves those who are earnest and persistent in supplication."[4]

Another ḥadīth mentions, "Each of you must ask his Lord for all his needs, even the strap of his sandal should it break."[5]

There are many ḥadīths having this meaning. There are also many

---

[3] Aḥmad #9701, Tirmidhī #3373, ibn Mājah #3827

Its isnād was ruled ḍa'īf by Dhahabī, *al-Mīzān*, vol. 4, pg. 538 and Arna'ūṭ et. al.

However the ḥadīth was ruled ḥasan due to supports by Albānī, *al-Ṣaḥīḥah* #2654

[4] Ṭabarānī, *al-Du'ā* #20, Bayhaqī, *Shu'ab al-Īmān* #1108, Quḍā'ī #1069 on the authority of 'Ā'ishah.

The ḥadīth is not recorded by Tirmidhī

Ibn 'Adī ruled it bāṭil as did Albānī, *al-Ḍa'īfah* #637 and he ruled it mawḍū' in *al-Irwā'* #677. cf. Ibn Ḥajr, *Talkhīs al-Ḥabīr* #716, 'Uqaylī, vol. 4, pg. 1554 #2085, ibn 'Adī, *al-Kāmil*, vol. 8, pg. 500-501

Bukhārī #6340 records the ḥadīth of Abū Hurayrah that the Messenger of Allāh (ﷺ) said, "Your supplications will be answered as long as you are not impatient by saying, 'I have supplicated to my Lord but He has not answered.'" Muslim #2735 records the ḥadīth of Abū Hurayrah that the Messenger of Allāh (ﷺ) said, "The supplication of the servant will always be answered provided that he does not supplicate for something sinful or supplicate to sever the ties of kinship and provided that he is not impatient." It was asked, "Messenger of Allāh, what is impatience?" He replied, "He says: 'I have supplicated and supplicated but I have not received an answer' then he becomes frustrated and leaves off supplicating."

[5] Tirmidhī #3682 on the authority of Anas and he said it was gharīb.

It was declared ḍa'īf by Albānī, *al-Ḍa'īfah* #1362

authentic ḥadīths prohibiting asking creation.

Ibn Mas'ūd reports that the Messenger of Allāh (ﷺ) said, "A person, despite being rich, will keep on asking until his face wears out and he will then not have a face with Allāh."[6]

The Prophet (ﷺ) took an oath of allegiance from a group of his Companions not to ask people for anything[7] amongst whom were Abū Bakr al-Ṣiddīq, Abū Dharr and Thawbān. If their whip or the muzzle of their camels fell down, they would not ask anyone to retrieve it for them.

Know that asking Allāh, Most High, rather than His creation is what is required, both from a rational and legal standpoint.

Asking is a form of sacrificing one's honour and humbling oneself to the petitioned, and that is only viable for Allāh. Humbling is only for Allāh through worship and request and is a sign of true love.

Yūsuf ibn al-Ḥusayn was asked, 'What is with the lovers that

---

[6] Bazzār #919, Ṭabarānī, *al-Kabir*, vol. 20, pg. 333 #790 on the authority of Mas'ūd ibn 'Amar and not ibn Mas'ūd

Ibn Abī Ḥātim, *al-Jarḥ wa'l-Ta'dīl*, vol. 8, pg. 282 said the ḥadīth was munkar.

Bukhārī #1474 and Muslim #1040 record on the authority of ibn 'Umar that the Prophet (ﷺ) said, "A person will keep asking of people until he will come on the Day of Rising devoid of a single morsel of flesh on his face."

Aḥmad #22420 and Bazzār #923 record on the authority of Thawbān that the Messenger of Allāh (ﷺ) said, "Whoever asks for something and is in no need of it, it will mar his face on the Day of Rising." Bazzār said the isnād was ḥasan and it was ruled ṣaḥīḥ by Arna'ūṭ et. al.

[7] Muslim #1043 on the authority of 'Awf ibn Mālik.

they take such delight in humbling themselves in love?' He replied,

> For love, a person's humility is nobility,
> Submissiveness to the beloved is dignity.

This act of humbling and this love is only valid for Allāh Alone, they are the components of true worship which is particular to the True God.

Imām Aḥmad, may Allāh have mercy on him, would say in his supplication, 'O Allāh! Just as you have prevented my face from prostrating to other than You, prevent it also from asking other than You!'

Abū'l-Khayr al-Aqṭa' said, 'I was in Mecca one year and was afflicted by harm and need, each time I went out to beg, a voice would cry out, "You would offer a face that prostrates to Me to someone else?!"'

In this sense, one of them said,

> One who offers Him his face
> when asking will never accept
> another in His place even if
> begging him brings affluence.
> Were you to weigh asking
> against any gifts conferred,
> Asking would preponderate
> and every gift secondary.
> If you must proffer
> your face by begging,

Offer it to the One
who is kind and generous.

It is for this reason that one who is given to begging without need will come on the Day of Rising without a morsel of flesh on his face as is established in the Two Ṣaḥīḥs.[8] This is because, in this world, he took away the nobility of his face, its sanctity and its honour, so Allāh, on the Day of Rising, will take away its physical beauty and grace, leaving a fleshless skeleton in its place. So too will He take away its inner beauty and grace and the person will be left having no status with Allāh.

Asking Allāh expresses servitude of a profound nature because in doing so, one displays his need of Him and acknowledges His ability of answering that need. To ask a created object is oppressive because that object is unable to procure good for itself, or repress harm from itself, let alone do so for another! To ask of it is to put something that is unable in the place of One who is able.

This meaning is testified to by the ḥadīth in Ṣaḥīḥ Muslim on the authority of Abū Dharr that the Prophet (ﷺ) said, "My servants! If the first and last of you, the man and Jinn of you, stood in one plain and asked of Me, and I granted every one his request, it would not decrease what is with Me except as a needle decreases the (volume) of an ocean when dipped in it."[9]

Tirmidhī and others record an additional wording, "...and that

[8] Bukhārī #1474 and Muslim #1040

[9] Muslim #2577

is because I am the generous, rich beyond need, glorious. I do what I wish. My gift is a word and My punishment is a word. When I wish a thing to be, I only say, 'Be!' and it is."[10]

So how can one who is needy and incapable be asked yet the One who is rich and able be left?! This is truly astonishing!

One of the Salaf said, 'I am ashamed to ask Allāh for anything of this world even though He owns it, so how can I possibly ask someone who does not own it?!' i.e. an object of creation.

One of the Salaf came upon difficult times and decided to ask one of his brothers for help. He saw a person in a dream saying,

Is it acceptable for one who is free,
When he finds all he wants with Allāh,
To incline his heart towards the servants?

he awoke to find that he was, amongst people, the most content of heart.

One of the Salaf said, 'I read the following in one of the heavenly scriptures: "Allāh, Mighty and Magnificent, says, 'Is someone other than Me hoped for during adversity?! Adversity is in My hand and I am the Ever-Living, the Self-Sustaining. Someone other than Me is hoped for and his door is knocked on in the early hours?! In My hands are the keys to all treasures and My door is open to whoever invokes Me! Who can say that he placed his hope in Me during hardship yet I cut him off? Who can say

[10] Aḥmad #21367-21369, Tirmidhī #2495, ibn Mājah #4257
Tirmidhī said it was ḥasan and Arna'ūṭ et. al. said it was ṣaḥīḥ due to witnesses.

that he placed his hope in Me during adversity and I cut short his hope? Who can say that he knocked on My door and I did not open it for him? I am the source of hopes, so how can hopes be severed before Me? Am I a miser such that the servant finds me niggardly? Is not the world, the Hereafter, kindness and grace entirely with Me? What prevents the hopers from placing their hope in Me? Were I to gather the inhabitants of the heavens and the earth and grant each and every one of them what I grant all of them together, and were I to fulfil the hope of each one of them, my dominion would not be decreased an atoms weight! How can a dominion decrease, the sustainer of which is Me? Wretched is the state of those who despair of My mercy, wretched is the state of those who disobey Me and boldly encroach My proscriptions!"'"

Allāh loves to be asked and is angry at someone who does not ask Him. He wants His servants to desire Him, to ask Him, to invoke Him and show their need of Him. He loves those who are earnest and persistent in supplication. Creation, generally, hates being asked because it is needy and incapable.

Ibn al-Sammāk said, 'Ask not one who will run away from you rather than listen to your request, instead ask One who has ordered you to ask Him.'

Abū'l-'Atāhiyyah said,

Allāh is angry if you leave asking Him,
The child of Ādam is angry when you ask him.
Direct your request to God since
In our Lords blessings do we vacillate.

Yaḥyā ibn Muʿādh would say, 'O You who are angry at whoever does not ask of You, do not hold back from someone who does ask You!'

Allāh, Most High, requests His servants to ask of Him. Every night He calls out, "Is there one asking of Me that I may give him? Is there one invoking Me that I may respond?"[11]

Allāh, Most High, says,

وَإِذَا سَأَلَكَ
عِبَادِي عَنِّي فَإِنِّي قَرِيبٌ أُجِيبُ دَعْوَةَ الدَّاعِ إِذَا دَعَانِ

"If My servants ask you about Me, I am near. I answer the call of the caller when he calls on Me."[12]

Regardless of what time the servant supplicated to Him, he will find Him hearing, close and responsive; there will be no screen between the two and no sentry at the door. Were he to ask a created being, quickly would he find barriers erected, doors being closed and he will find it very difficult to reach the person most of the time.

[11] Bukhārī #1145-6321-7494 and Muslim #756 record on the authority of Abū Hurayrah that the Prophet (ﷺ) said, "Every night, when the last third of the night remains, our Lord, Blessed and Most High, descends to the lowest heaven and says, 'Is there anyone invoking Me that I may respond? Is there anyone asking of Me that I may give it to him? Is there anyone who asking My forgiveness that I may forgive him?'"

[12] *al-Baqarah* (2): 186

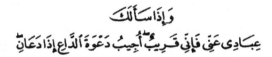

Ṭāwus said to 'Aṭā', 'Beware of seeking your needs from one who would shut the door in your face and erect a barrier. Instead, go to One whose door is open till the Day of Judgment, who has ordered you to ask of Him and has promised you to respond.'[13]

Wahb ibn Munabbih said to one of the scholars, 'Have I not been informed that you go to kings and the sons of kings (selling) your knowledge to them? Woe to you! You go to one who would close his door in your face and make out that he is poor, hiding his richness, and you leave One who has opened His door for you at midday and midnight and shows His richness to you saying, "Invoke Me and I will respond"?!'

Maymūn ibn Mihrān saw some people gathering at the door of one of the rulers and remarked, 'Whoever's need is not fulfilled by the Sulṭān should know that the houses of the All-Merciful are always open. Let him go to the Masjid and pray two rak'ahs and ask Him for his need.'

Bakr al-Muzani would say, 'Son of Ādam, who is there like you! Whenever you wish you can purify yourself and privately discourse with your Lord with no barrier between you and no need for a translator.'

A man asked one of the righteous to intercede for him in getting his request answered by someone. He said, 'I will not leave a door that is open to go instead to a door that is closed.'

In this respect, one of them said,

---

[13] Abū Nu'aym, vol. 4, pg. 11, vol. 8, pg. 141

The courtyards of kings are barred
Allāh's door is open, unbarred.

Another said,

Say to those hiding from the petitioners
In houses that are barred approach,
Should the sentries prevent your entry,
'At His door, Allāh has no sentry.'

Another said to one of the scholars,

Sit not at the door of one
Who would refuse you entry.
You reason: My need will remain
Unmet if I do not visit his house.
Leave him; go instead to its Lord,
It will be met, the former begrudging!

Ibn Abī al-Dunyā[14] records the ḥadīth of Abū 'Ubaydah ibn 'Abdullāh ibn Mas'ūd that a man came to the Prophet (ﷺ) and said, 'Messenger of Allāh, Banū so-and-so have attacked me and taken my son and camels.' The Prophet (ﷺ) said, "The family of Muḥammad live in such-and-such a place, they do not even possess a *mudd* or *ṣā'* of food, so ask Allāh, Mighty and Magnificent." He returned to his wife and she asked, 'What did he say to you?' so he told her. She said, 'What an excellent response!' It was not long after that Allāh returned his son to him along with more camels than he had in the first place! He then came to the Prophet (ﷺ) and told him of what had happened, so the Prophet (ﷺ)

[14] Ibn Abī al-Dunyā, *al-Faraj ba'd al-Shidda*, pg. 10, and *al-Qanā'ah wa'l-Ta'affuf*, pg. 54; Bayhaqī, *al-Dalā'il*, vol. 6, pg. 107

ascended the pulpit and praised Allāh, eulogising Him. Then he ordered the people to ask of Allāh, Mighty and Magnificent, and to place their desire in Him. He recited,

وَمَن يَتَّقِ ٱللَّهَ يَجْعَل لَّهُۥ مَخْرَجًا ۝٢ وَيَرْزُقْهُ مِنْ حَيْثُ لَا يَحْتَسِبُ

"Whoever has *taqwā* of Allāh - He will give him a way out and provide for him from where he does not expect."[15]

A man asked Thābit al-Bunānī to intercede for him with a judge in order that a particular need of his be met. Thābit stood to go with him and each time he passed by a Masjid on the way, he entered, prayed and supplicated. When they finally reached the court, the Judge had left. The petitioner set about blaming him and he said, 'All this while, I have only been responding to your need!' Allāh fulfilled his need without his needing to go to the judge.

Once, while Isḥāq ibn 'Ubbād al-Baṣrī was sleeping, he saw a person in a dream saying, 'Relieve one who is overly anxious!' When he awoke he asked, 'Is there anyone needy in the neighbourhood?' They replied, 'We don't know.' Then he slept and the same dream occurred a second time, and then a third time with the man saying, 'You are sleeping without relieving him?!' He awoke and, taking three hundred dirhams with him, rode his mule to Baṣra. There he stopped at the door of a Masjid which was holding some funeral prayers. He entered and saw a man praying, when the man realised he was there, he completed his prayer and came to him. (Isḥāq) said, 'O servant of Allāh!

[15] *al-Ṭalāq* (65): 2

(What are you doing) at this time and in this place? What do you need?' He replied, 'I am man who possesses only one hundred dirhams which I have lost, and I also have a debt of two hundred dirhams.' He took out his money and said, 'Here is three hundred dirhams, take them.' He took them and then (Isḥāq) asked, 'Do you know me?' He replied, 'No.' He said, 'I am Isḥāq ibn 'Ubbād and should you face adversity, come to me, my house is in such-and-such a place.' He replied, 'May Allāh have mercy on you! If adversity afflicts us, we will resort to the One who brought you here to us in the first place!'

'Abdu'l-Raḥmān ibn Zayd ibn Aslam said, 'One morning, my mother said to my father, "By Allāh, there is no meat at all to eat in this house of yours!" He stood, performed ablution, put on his usual clothes and prayed in the house. My mother turned to me and said, "Your father will do no more than this, so you go." I left and a friend of ours who sold dates came to mind so I went to his market. When he saw me he called me, took me to his house and fed me. Then, out of his own volition, without my saying anything about our difficulty, he took out a purse containing thirty dīnārs and said, "Convey my greeting to your father and tell him that we have made him a partner in our business and that this is his share."'

Ibrāhīm ibn Adham left for a military expedition with some of his colleagues. They decided to share the expenses and each person gave his share, he started thinking about which of his companions he could take a loan from, then came to himself and wept saying, 'Woe to me! I seek from the servants and leave their Master?! He says to me, "Who is more deserving of your request, them or Me?"' He performed ablution, prayed two rak'ahs, and when in prostration said, 'My Lord! You know what I have done and that it was done out of error and ignorance. If You were to punish me, I deserve it, and if You were to pardon me, You can do so. You know well my need so fulfil it by Your mercy!' He raised his head to find some four hundred dīnārs with him, from those he took one dīnār and left.

Aṣbagh ibn Zayd said, 'I and those with me went three days without eating anything. My two young daughters came to me and cried, "O father! We are hungry!" So I went to the basin of water, performed ablution, prayed two rak'ahs, and I was inspired to say a certain supplication, the last words of which were, "O Allāh, open the gates of provision for me and let me not be indebted to anyone in its grant, nor make me to be responsible to You in the Hereafter, concerning it, by Your mercy, O Most Merciful of the merciful." I went back to the house and my oldest daughter stood and said, "Father, my uncle just came with this purse containing dirhams, this carrier laden with flour and this carrier laden with everything in the Market! He said, 'Convey my greetings to my brother and tell him that whenever he is in need, he should supplicate with that supplication and his need will be met.'"' Aṣbagh then said, 'By Allāh, I do not have a brother and I did not know who the person was, however Allāh is omnipotent!'

Ḥakam ibn Mūsā said, 'I woke up one morning and my wife complained about not having any flour or bread. I left knowing that I would be unable to get anything and while walking down the street I said, "O Allāh! You know that I know that You know that I have no flour or bread or money, so grant them to us!" A man met me and asked, "Do you wish bread or flour?" I replied, "Either." Then I walked around during the day trying to find means to acquire what I needed but was unable. When I returned home my family had prepared a veritable feast of bread and meat.

I asked, "Where did you get this?" They replied, "From the person you sent!" I remained silent.'

Awzā'ī said, 'While performing *ṭawāf*, I saw a man clinging onto the sheets of the Ka'bah saying, "My Lord! You see that I am poor. You see my children naked. You see my camel emaciated. So what see You, O one who sees and is not seen!" A voice called out behind him saying, "'Āṣim, Āṣim, go to your uncle, he has passed away at Tā'if and left behind him one thousand ewes, three hundred camels, four hundred dirhams, four slaves and three Yemeni swords. Go and take them for you are his only inheritor!" I said, "'Āṣim, the one you were invoking was close to you!" He said, "Have you not heard His, Most High, saying,

وَإِذَا سَأَلَكَ
عِبَادِى عَنِّى فَإِنِّى قَرِيبٌ أُجِيبُ دَعْوَةَ ٱلدَّاعِ إِذَا دَعَانِ

"If My servants ask you about Me, I am near. I answer the call of the caller when he calls on Me." '"[16]

The narrations and incidents concerning this are many and mentioning them would make this treatise very lengthy. They can be read in works such as *al-Faraj ba'd al-Shiddah* and *Mujābī al-Da'wah* of ibn Abī al-Dunyā, *Kitāb al-Mustaṣrikhīna bi'Allāhi 'inda Nuzūli'l-Balā'* of Qāḍī Abū'l-Walīd ibn al-Ṣaffār, *Kitāb al-Mustaghīthīna bi'Allāh 'inda Nuzūli'l-Balā'* of Ḥāfiẓ Abū'l-Qāsim ibn Bashkwāl al-Andulūsī and other works dealing with asceticism, heart melting issues and history.

Shaykh Abū'l-Faraj records in his major work on history, with

[16] *al-Baqarah* (2): 186

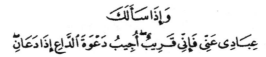

his chain of narration to Ḥasan ibn Sufyān al-Fasawī that he was residing in Egypt with a group of his colleagues, writing ḥadīth. They were in need so they sold their possessions to meet them, eventually they had nothing left to sell and were forced to go hungry for three days being unable to find anything to eat. They woke up on the fourth day having decided to beg because of their dire need. They drew lots to decide who would go begging and it fell on Ḥasan ibn Sufyān. He said, 'I felt confused and dismayed and could not resolve myself to beg.' Instead I went to the prayer area of the Masjid and prayed two long rak'ahs in which I supplicated to Allāh, Mighty and Magnificent, to relieve us of our adversity. I had not yet finished my prayer when a man entered the Masjid with his servant who has carrying a cloth. He asked, 'Who here is called Ḥasan ibn Sufyān?' I raised my head from prostration and replied, 'I am.' He said, 'Amīr ibn Ṭūlūn conveys his greetings to you and welcomes you. He asks your forgiveness for not keeping up with your affairs and not fulfilling your rights. He has sent you all that you would need to meet your expenses. He himself will visit you tomorrow and ask to be excused by yourselves.' He placed in the hands of every one of us a purse containing one hundred dirhams. We were astounded and asked him how this had happened. He said, 'He was sleeping today and in his dream saw a knight in the sky saying, "Stand and go to Ḥasan ibn Sufyan and his companions in the Masjid of so-and-so for they have gone hungry these past three days!" He asked, "Who are you?" He replied, "I am Riḍwān, the guardian of Paradise!"' Ḥasan said, 'We thanked Allāh, Mighty and Magnificent, then we made ready our belongings, set things right and left Egypt that same night out for fear that the Amīr may actually visit us and, as result, we gain fame and status amongst the masses leading to ostentation and pomposity.'

He also records with his isnād to Muḥammad ibn Hārūn al-Ruwayānī that he and Muḥammad ibn Naṣr al-Marwazī, Muḥammad ibn 'Ulwayh al-Warrāq, and Muḥammad ibn Isḥāq ibn Khuzaymah all met together, and he mentioned the same story as above in meaning, and he mentioned that the supplicant was actually ibn Khuzaymah. He records via another isnād that they were four and they were Muḥammad ibn Jarīr, Muḥammad ibn Naṣr, Muḥammad ibn Khuzaymah and Muḥammad ibn Hārūn.

CHAPTER SIX

Seeking Allāh's Help

The Messenger of Allāh (ﷺ) said, "When you seek aid, turn to Allāh." After ordering us to safeguard Allāh and to know Him in times of ease - this being the very essence of worship, he directed us to ask Allāh Alone and to invoke Him: "Du'ā is worship," as is mentioned in the ḥadīth of Nu'mān ibn Bashīr, and after stating this, the Prophet (ﷺ) recited,

وَقَالَ رَبُّكُمُ ادْعُونِي أَسْتَجِبْ لَكُمْ

"Your Lord says, 'Call on Me and I will answer you.'"[1]

This was recorded by the authors of the Four Sunans.[2]

---

[1] *Ghāfir* (40): 60

[2] Abū Dāwūd #1479, Tirmidhī #2969-3247-3372, Nasā'ī, *al-Kubrā* #11464, ibn Mājah #3828

Tirmidhī said it was ḥasan ṣaḥīḥ. Nawawī, *al-Adhkār*, pg. 478 said its isnād was ṣaḥīḥ, ibn Ḥajr, *Fatḥ*, vol. 1, pg. 64 said that its isnād was jayyid, ibn Ḥibbān #2396 ruled it ṣaḥīḥ as did Ḥākim #1902 with Dhahabī agreeing. Albānī, *Ṣaḥīḥ al-Targhīb* #1627 said it was ṣaḥīḥ.

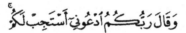

After all this, he directed us to seek the aid of Allāh Alone, and this is derived from His saying,

إِيَّاكَ نَعْبُدُ وَإِيَّاكَ نَسْتَعِينُ ۝٥

"You alone we worship and You alone we ask for help."[3]

This verse lays out a comprehensive principle and it is said that the essential message of all revealed scripture revolves around it.

There are two benefits in seeking the aid of Allāh Alone:

1) The servant does not have the strength to perform actions of obedience without Allāh's help.

2) There is none who can aid him in the betterment of his worldly and religious life except for Allāh, Mighty and Magnificent. Whoever Allāh helps is truly aided and whoever Allāh forsakes is truly forsaken.

The authentic ḥadīth mentions that the Prophet (ﷺ) said, "Be desirous of all that would benefit you and seek Allāh's aid and do not despair."[4]

He (ﷺ) would say in his sermons, and teach his Companions to say, "All praise is due to Allāh, we ask for His aid and seek His guidance...."[5]

---

[3] *al-Fātiḥah* (1): 5

[4] Muslim #2664 on the authority of Abū Hurayrah.

[5] Shāfi'ī, *Musnad*, vol. 1, pg. 147 on the authority of ibn 'Abbās with a ḍa'īf =

He ordered Mu'ādh to never leave saying, "O Allāh! Aid me in remembering You, being grateful to You and making good my worship of You" at the end of every prayer.[6]

One of his (ﷺ) supplications was, "My Lord! Aid me and do not aid others against me!"[7]

The supplication of Qunūt which was employed by 'Umar and others mentioned, "O Allāh! We seek Your aid!"[8]

A famous narration mentions that, after striking the sea to make it split, Mūsā (*'alayhis-salām*) said, 'O Allāh! To You belongs all praise, to You does one complain, You are the One whose aid is sought, and to You does one turn for relief, in You does one place his trust, and there is no might or motion except with You.'[9]

=

jiddan isnād.

The sermon, without the words, "seek His guidance," is recorded by Muslim.

[6] Aḥmad #22119-22126, Abū Dāwūd #1522, Nasā'ī #1304 and *'Amal al-Yawm wa'l-Laylah* #109

Nawawī, *al-Adhkār*, pg. 103, *al-Khulāṣah*, vol. 1, pg. 468, *Riyāḍ* #389-1430 said that the isnād was ṣaḥīḥ, as did ibn Kathīr, *al-Bidāyah*, vol. 7, pg. 97. Ibn 'Allān, *al-Futūḥāt al-Rabbāniyyah*, vol. 3, pg. 55 quotes ibn Ḥajr saying it was ṣaḥīḥ. Albānī, *Ṣaḥīḥ al-Targhīb* #1596 said it was ṣaḥīḥ as did Arna'ūṭ.

[7] Aḥmad #1997, Abū Dāwūd #1510-1511, Tirmidhī #3551

Tirmidhī said it was ḥasan ṣaḥīḥ. It was ruled ṣaḥīḥ by ibn Ḥibbān #948 and Ḥākim #1910 with Dhahabī agreeing. Albānī, *Ṣaḥīḥ al-Tirmidhī* ruled it ṣaḥīḥ and Arna'ūṭ said the isnād was ṣaḥīḥ.

[8] Ṭaḥāwī, *Ma'ānī al-Āthār*, vol. 1, pg. 250 with a jayyid isnād.

[9] Ṭabarānī, *al-Awsaṭ*, *al-Ṣaghīr* on the authority of ibn Mas'ūd.

Haythamī, vol. 10, pg. 183 said, 'Its isnād contains narrators I do not know.'

The servant is in need of seeking Allāh's aid in performing the prescribed and abandoning the proscribed, and in bearing the vicissitudes of decree with patience. Ya'qūb (*'alayhis-salām*) said,

فَصَبْرٌ جَمِيلٌ وَٱللَّهُ ٱلْمُسْتَعَانُ عَلَىٰ مَا تَصِفُونَ ﴿١٨﴾

"...but beauty lies in showing patience and it is Allāh alone who is my Help in the face of what you describe."[10]

It is for this reason that 'Ā'ishah said this same statement in the incident of the Lie and Allāh cleared her of the false accusation.

Mūsā said to his people,

ٱسْتَعِينُوا۟ بِٱللَّهِ وَٱصْبِرُوٓا۟

"So seek help in Allāh and be patient."[11]

Allāh said to his Prophet (ﷺ),

قَٰلَ
رَبِّ ٱحْكُم بِٱلْحَقِّ وَرَبُّنَا ٱلرَّحْمَٰنُ ٱلْمُسْتَعَانُ عَلَىٰ مَا تَصِفُونَ ﴿١١٢﴾

"Say: 'Lord, judge with truth! Our Lord is the All-Merciful and the One whose help is sought in the face of what you describe!'"[12]

---

[10] *Yūsuf* (12): 18

[11] *al-A'rāf* (7): 128

[12] *al-Anbiyā'* (21): 112

When the Prophet (ﷺ) gave 'Uthmān the good news that he would enter Paradise after going through tribulation, he said, "Allāh's aid is sought!"[13] When they entered on 'Uthmān and beat him, with blood pouring down his body, he was saying, '*None has the right to be worshipped save You, Glory be to You, I have been one of the wrong-doers.* O Allāh! I take refuge with You against them, I seek Your aid in all my affairs, and I ask You for the patience to bear what You have tested me with!'

It is reported on the authority of Abū Ṭalḥah that the Prophet (ﷺ) said in one of his battles when encountering the enemy, "O Master of the Day of Judgment, it is You we worship and Your aid we seek!" Abū Ṭalḥah said, 'I saw the men falling down in fits!'[14] This was recorded by Abū'l-Shaykh al-Aṣbahānī.

The servant is in need of seeking Allāh's aid in acquiring good in his religious and worldly life as Zubayr said in his final advice to his son, 'Abdullāh, asking him to pay off his debts, 'If you are unable, seek the help of my Master.' He asked, 'Father, who is your master?' He replied, 'Allāh.' He said, 'Whenever I found it difficult to pay off his debts, I said, "Master of Zubayr, pay off his debt!" and it would be paid off.'

In the first sermon that 'Umar ibn al-Khaṭṭāb (*raḍiyAllāhu 'anhu*) delivered off the pulpit he said, 'The Arabs are like a long suffering camel[15] whose muzzle I have taken hold of, I will take it

[13] Muslim #2403

[14] Ṭabarānī, *al-Awsaṭ* #8163 and ibn al-Sunnī, *'Amal al-Yawm wa'l-Laylah* #334 Haythamī, vol. 5, pg. 328 said that its isnād contained 'Abdu'l-Salām ibn Hāshim who is ḍa'īf. It was ruled ḍa'īf by Albānī, *al-Ḍa'īfah* #5105

[15] i.e. it endures any pain it faces and does what it has to do.

across the great plain and I seek the aid of Allāh in doing so.'

The servant will also need Allāh's help to get him through the terrors of the Day of Rising: from the point of his death onwards.

When Khālid ibn al-Walīd was on his death bed, one of the men around him said, 'It is something terribly hard,' i.e. death. Khalid said, 'Certainly! But I seek the aid of Allāh, Mighty and Magnificent.'

When 'Āmir ibn 'Abdullāh ibn al-Zubayr was on his death bed, he cried and said, 'I am only crying at (losing) the heat of the day and the coolness of the standing,' i.e. fasting during the day and praying by night. He said, 'I seek Allāh's aid in bearing this fatal injury of mine.'

One of the early people said, 'My Lord! I am amazed at how someone who knows You could hope in another! I am amazed at how someone who knows You could seek help from another.'

al-Ḥasan wrote to 'Umar ibn 'Abdu'l-'Azīz, may Allāh have mercy on him, 'Do not seek the aid of any besides Allāh or Allāh may leave you to him.'

One of them said, 'Seek the aid of Allāh, seek His aid for He is the best of those whose aid is sought.'

CHAPTER SEVEN

The Pens have Dried

He (ﷺ) said, "The Pen has dried (after having written) all that will occur," and in another narration, "The Pens have been lifted and the books have dried," and in another narration, "The Pens have been lifted and the scrolls have dried."

All of these statements serve as a metonymy (*kināyah*) referring to the workings of the decree and to the fact that they have all been recorded in an erstwhile, comprehensive book. It is said about a book that has been completed a long time ago: the pens have been lifted from it, or the pens employed to write it have dried, or the page has dried. This is a fine way of alluding to the decree and lends to a greater sense of gravity.

The Book and authentic Sunnah also point to this meaning. Allāh, Mighty and Magnificent, says,

مَآ أَصَابَ
مِن مُّصِيبَةٍ فِى ٱلْأَرْضِ وَلَا فِىٓ أَنفُسِكُمْ إِلَّا فِى كِتَٰبٍ
مِّن قَبْلِ أَن نَّبْرَأَهَآ ۚ إِنَّ ذَٰلِكَ عَلَى ٱللَّهِ يَسِيرٌ ﴿٢٢﴾

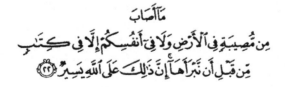

> **"Nothing occurs, either in the earth or in yourselves, without its being in a Book before We make it happen. That is something easy for Allāh."**[1]

Ḍaḥḥak reported that ibn 'Abbās said, 'Allāh created the Pen and commanded it to move by His leave. The size of the Pen is as the expanse between heaven and earth. The Pen said, "Lord, what shall I write?" He said, "Everything that I am to create and everything that will occur in My creation: rain, plant, soul, deed, provision or life-span." The Pen then wrote everything that was to occur until the Day of Rising and Allāh placed it in a Book inscribed under the Throne, with Him.'

Abū Ẓabyān reported that ibn 'Abbās said, 'The first thing that Allāh created was the Pen which He commanded, "Write!" It asked, "What shall I write?" He replied, "The decree." It then recorded all that was to happen until the Last Hour is established.' Then he recited,

نٓ وَٱلْقَلَمِ وَمَا يَسْطُرُونَ ۝١

"Nūn. By the Pen and what they write down."[2]

Abū'l-Ḍuḥā narrated something similar from ibn 'Abbās.[3] The

---

[1] *al-Ḥadīd* (57): 22

[2] *al-Qalam* (68): 1-2
The narration is in Ṭabarī (in exegesis to 68:1), Ājurrī, *al-Sharī'ah* #183-350 with a ṣaḥīḥ isnād. It was ruled ṣaḥīḥ by Ḥākim #3840 with Dhahabī agreeing.

[3] Ibid., Ājurrī #182 and it is ṣaḥīḥ.

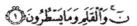

narration of Abū'l-Ḍuḥā is also narrated as a ḥadīth of the Messenger (ﷺ) but it is not authentic.[4]

Ibn Baṭṭah records, with a ḍa'īf isnād, on the authority of Abū Hurayrah that the Prophet (ﷺ) said, "The first thing that Allāh created was the Pen, and after it, al-Nūn which is an inkpot. He commanded, 'Write!' It asked, 'What should I write?' He said, 'Write everything that will happen until the Day of Rising.' That is the saying of Allāh, Mighty and Magnificent,

ٓنٓۚ وَٱلْقَلَمِ وَمَا يَسْطُرُونَ ۝١

"Nūn. By the Pen and what they write down."[5]

Then the Pen was sealed such that it cannot speak and it will not speak until the Day of Rising."[6]

Imām Aḥmad, Abū Dāwūd and Tirmidhī record the ḥadīth of 'Ubādah ibn al-Ṣāmit that the Prophet (ﷺ) said, "The first thing

---

[4] Ṭabarānī, *al-Kabīr* #12227.

The isnād is ḍa'īf as it contains the narrator Mu'ammal ibn Ismā'īl who is truthful but of poor memory. Haythamī, vol. 7, pg. 128 said, 'Mu'ammal is trustworthy but makes many mistakes. Ibn Ma'īn and others said that he was thiqah while Bukhārī and others said he was ḍa'īf.'

[5] *al-Qalam* (68): 1-2

The narration is Ṭabarī, vol. 29, pp. 9-10

[6] Ibn Baṭṭah, *al-Ibānah (Qadr)* #1364, Ājurrī #179-345. Suyūṭī, *al-La'i al-Maṣnū'ah*, vol. 1, pg. 131 references it to Ḥakīm al-Tirmidhī and it is also recorded by ibn 'Asākir, *Tārikh al-Dimashq*, vol. 17, pg. 247.

Ibn 'Adī, *al-Kāmil*, vol. 7, pg. 522 #1753 said the ḥadīth was bāṭil and munkar and Dhahabī, *al-Mīzān*, vol. 4, pg. 61 #8298 agreed as did Albānī, *al-Ḍa'īfah* #1253.

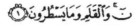

that Allāh created was the Pen which He commanded, 'Write!' In that hour it recorded all that was to happen until the Day of Rising."[7]

Muslim records on the authority of 'Abdullāh ibn 'Amr that the Prophet (ﷺ) said, "Allāh recorded the fates of all creatures fifty thousand years before He created the heavens and the earth."[8]

Imām Aḥmad, Tirmidhī and Nasā'ī record the ḥadīth of 'Abdullāh ibn 'Amr who said, 'The Messenger of Allāh (ﷺ) came out to us carrying two books. He asked, "Do you know what these books are?" We replied, 'Messenger of Allāh, no, not unless you tell us.' About the book that was in his right hand he said, "This is a book from the Lord of the worlds containing the names of the inhabitants of Paradise, the names of their parents and their tribes (in detail). It is completed to the last man and they will not increase in number, nor decrease in number." About the book in his left hand he said, "This is a book from the Lord of the worlds containing the names of the denizens of the Fire, the names of their parents and their tribes (in detail). It is completed to the last man and they will not increase in number or decrease in number." His Companions asked, "Messenger of Allāh, if the affair is already decided, why work deeds?" He replied, "Remain firm, steadfast and balanced. The last act of an inhabitant of Paradise will be a deed of the people of Paradise no matter what he may have done, and the last act of a denizen

---

[7] Aḥmad #22705-22707, Abū Dāwūd #4700, Tirmidhī #2155-3319.
Tirmidhī said it was ḥasan ṣaḥīḥ gharīb and it was ruled ṣaḥīḥ by ibn al-'Arabī, *Aḥkām al-Qur'ān*, vol. 2, pg. 335, Albānī, *Ṣaḥīḥah* #133 and Arna'ūṭ.

[8] Muslim #2653

of the Fire will be a deed of the people of the Fire no matter what he may have done." Then the Messenger of Allāh (ﷺ) gestured with his hands, dropping the books, "Your Lord has decided everything about the servants: *'one group is for Paradise and one group is for the Blazing Fire!'*[9]"[10]

Imām Aḥmad records the ḥadīth of Abū'l-Dardā' that the Prophet (ﷺ) said, "Allāh has decided five matters for every servant: his lifespan, his provision, his deeds, his lying down, and whether he is wretched or felicitous."[11]

Imām Aḥmad and Tirmidhī record the ḥadīth of ibn Mas'ūd that the Prophet (ﷺ) said, "Allāh created every soul and decreed its life, its provision and the tribulations it would face."[12]

---

[9] *al-Shūrā* (42): 7

[10] Aḥmad #6563, Tirmidhī #2141, Nasā'ī, *al-Kubrā* #11409

Tirmidhī said it was ḥasan ṣaḥīḥ gharīb and Nasā'ī said it was ṣaḥīḥ as mentioned in *Tuḥfatu'l-Ashrāf*, vol. 6, pg. 243. Ibn Ḥajr, *Fatḥ*, vol. 6, pg. 336 said the isnād was ḥasan as did Albānī, *al-Ṣaḥīḥah* #848.

[11] Aḥmad #21722 with the words, "Allāh has decided five matters for every servant: his lifespan, his deeds, his resting, his moving about and his provision." It was ruled ṣaḥīḥ by ibn Ḥibbān #6150

Aḥmad #21723 with the words, "Allāh has decided five matters for every servant: his lifespan, his provision, his deeds, and whether he is wretched or felicitous." Suyūṭī, *al-Jāmi' al-Ṣaghīr* #5848 said it was ṣaḥīḥ as did Wādi'ī, *al-Ṣaḥīḥ al-Musnad* #1045

Albānī, *Ẓilāl al-Jannah* #307-308 and Arna'ūṭ ruled both to be ṣaḥīḥ.

[12] Aḥmad #4197, Tirmidhī #2143

Albānī, *al-Ṣaḥīḥah* #1152 and Arna'ūṭ said it was ṣaḥīḥ.

Aḥmad #8343 records on the authority of Abū Hurayrah that the Messenger

=

Muslim records the ḥadīth of Jābir that a man asked the Messenger of Allāh (ﷺ), 'Messenger of Allāh, what is the purpose of the deeds done today, are they for matters concerning which the pens have dried and fates have been decided, or for something in our future?' He replied, "Rather concerning something which the pens have dried and fates have been decided." He asked, 'Then why work deeds?' He replied, "Do your deeds for everyone is eased (towards what he was created for)."[13]

There are a great many aḥādīth that convey this meaning and so too narrations from the Companions. One of them said,

Commit the affair wholly (to the Owner)
The Pen has dried, writing all that will occur.
Man has such a Creator,
None can avert His decree or order.

=

of Allāh (ﷺ) said, "Allāh created every soul and decreed its life, its death, the tribulations it would face and its provision." It was declared ṣaḥīḥ by ibn Ḥibbān #6118-6119 and Arna'ūṭ.

[13] Muslim #2648

CHAPTER EIGHT

Only Allāh's Decree is in Effect

The Messenger of Allāh (ﷺ) said, "If the whole of creation, in its entirety, was to try and effectuate some benefit for you through something that Allāh has not decreed, they would not be able to do so; and if they wished to harm you through something that Allāh has not prescribed, they would not be able to do so."

What is meant is that every harm or benefit that the servant encounters in this world is already decreed for him, it is impossible for him to face anything that has not been decreed for him even if the whole of creation strove their utmost in bringing it about. The Qur'ān also proves this in verses such as:

قُل لَّن يُصِيبَنَآ إِلَّا مَا كَتَبَ ٱللَّهُ لَنَا

"Say: 'Nothing can happen to us except what Allāh has ordained for us...'"[1]

---

[1] *al-Tawbah* (9): 51

مَآ أَصَابَ مِن مُّصِيبَةٍ فِى ٱلْأَرْضِ وَلَا فِىٓ أَنفُسِكُمْ إِلَّا فِى كِتَٰبٍ مِّن قَبْلِ أَن نَّبْرَأَهَآ ۚ إِنَّ ذَٰلِكَ عَلَى ٱللَّهِ يَسِيرٌ ﴿٢٢﴾

"Nothing occurs, either in the earth or in your selves, without its being in a Book before We make it happen..."[2]

قُل لَّوْ كُنتُمْ فِى بُيُوتِكُمْ لَبَرَزَ ٱلَّذِينَ كُتِبَ عَلَيْهِمُ ٱلْقَتْلُ إِلَىٰ مَضَاجِعِهِمْ

"Say: 'Even if you have been inside your homes, those people for whom killing was decreed would have gone out to their place of death.'"[3]

Imām Aḥmad records the ḥadīth of Abū'l-Dardā' that the Prophet (ﷺ) said, "Everything has a reality and the servant will not attain the reality of faith until he knows that what afflicted him would never have missed him, and what missed him would never have afflicted him."[4] Abū Dāwūd and ibn Mājah record a ḥadīth of similar meaning on the authority of Zayd ibn Thābit.[5]

---

[2] *al-Ḥadīd* (57): 22

[3] *Āli 'Imrān* (3): 154

[4] Aḥmad #27490, ibn Abī 'Āṣim #246.
It was ruled ḥasan by Suyūṭī, *al-Jāmi'* #2417 and Wadi'ī, *Ṣaḥīḥ al-Musnad* #1050. Albānī, *Ẓilāl al-Jannah* #246, *al-Ṣaḥīḥah* #2471 ruled it ṣaḥīḥ due to supporting witnesses.

[5] Aḥmad #21589-21611-21653, Abū Dāwūd #4699, ibn Mājah #77 with the =

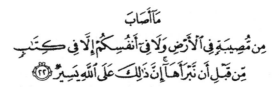

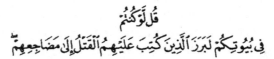

Know that this whole advice given to ibn 'Abbās revolves around this core principle and branches off from it. When the servant realises that he will encounter no good or evil, nor benefit or harm unless Allāh has first ordained it for him, when he realises that if the whole of creation strove their utmost in trying to effectuate something other than His decree, their efforts would be wholly ineffectual, he will then recognise that Allāh alone is the one who brings about benefit and causes harm, and that He alone is the one who grants and the one who withholds. This recognition will lead the servant to perfect the *Tawḥīd* of his Lord, Mighty and Magnificent. He will ask Him alone for help, he will entreat Him alone, and He will submit and humble himself before Him alone. And he will worship Him alone and obey Him alone. This is because something is worshipped in the hope that it will promote good or repress harm and it is for this reason that Allāh has censured those who worship objects that can promote no benefit and cause no harm, the worship of whom is of no use

=

words, "Were you to spend the likes of Uḥud in the Way of Allāh, Allāh would not accept it from you until you believe in the decree and you know that what afflicted you would never have missed you and what missed you would never have afflicted you. Were you to die on a (belief) other than this you would enter the Fire." It was ruled ṣaḥīḥ by ibn Ḥibbān #727, Albānī, *Takhrīj Abū Dāwūd* #4699, and Arna'ūṭ said that its isnād was strong.

Ibn Abī 'Āṣim #247 records on the authority of Anas that the Messenger of Allāh (ﷺ) said, "A servant will not experience the sweetness of faith until he knows that what afflicted him would never have missed him and what missed him would never have afflicted him." Albānī, *Ẓilāl al-Jannah* #247 said the isnād was ḥasan.

Tirmidhī #2144 and Ṭabarānī, *al-Kabīr* #11243 record on the authority of ibn 'Abbās that the Prophet (ﷺ) said, "A servant will not believe until he believes in the decree - the good and bad thereof: until he knows that what afflicted him would never have missed him and what missed him would never have afflicted him." It was ruled ṣaḥīḥ by Albānī, *al-Ṣaḥīḥah* #2439

at all.[6]

Many of those who have not actualised the reality of faith in their hearts actually put obedience to creatures before obedience to the Creator in the hope that they can grant them some benefit or repress some harm from them. When the servant truly realises that it is only Allāh who can bring about benefit, cause or remove harm, and grant or withhold, this will necessitate his singling Him out for obedience and worship and giving that precedence over obeying any other creature. It will also necessitate singling Him, Glorious is He, out alone when asking for help and for entreaty.

This comprehensive, magnificent legacy makes mention of all of these matters, each one of paramount importance.

A servant' safeguarding Allāh, Mighty and Magnificent, is a reference to his safeguarding His limits and carefully fulfilling His rights, this being the reality of worshipping Him. This is what this legacy commences with. This then leads to Allāh safeguarding the servant, the fruition of which is every servant's aim and objective.

Mentioned next is knowing Allāh in times of ease and that this leads to Allāh knowing His servant in times of difficulty: this is

[6] For example in the sayings of Allāh, **"They worship, instead of Allāh, what can neither harm them nor help them."** [*Yūnus* (10): 18], **"Yet they worship instead of Allāh what can neither help nor harm them."** [*al-Furqān* (25) :55], **"Father, why do worship what can neither hear nor see and is not of any use to you at all?"** [*Maryam* (19): 42], **"But they have adopted gods apart from Him which do not create anything but are themselves created. They have no power to harm or help themselves. They have no power over death or life or resurrection."** [*al-Furqān* (25) :3]

part and parcel of Allāh's safeguarding His servant and completes it. Times of difficulty have been specifically mentioned here because, on such occasions, the servants are in dire need of recoursing to one who knows them and can relieve them. At such times, even the polytheists make their supplication sincerely to Him alone, begging Him, imploring Him, knowing that only He, Glorious is He, can remove the harm facing them. However, when relieved, they revert to their polytheism as Allāh has mentioned in numerous places in His Book, and censured them for.[7] The Prophet (ﷺ), in this advice, has effectively ordered us to oppose their practice by knowing Allāh in times of ease through sincerely making the religion for Him alone, by obeying Him alone and seeking to draw close to Him alone. This will then necessitate His knowing them in times of hardship and relieving them of it.

Mentioned next is asking of Allāh alone and seeking His help alone. This subsumes both times of ease and times of hardship.

Next is mentioned the principle upon which all of what has preceded is built: Allāh, Most High, being alone in effectuating

[7] For example the sayings of Allāh, **"When harm touches man, he calls on Us, lying on his side or sitting down or standing up. Then when We remove the harm from him he carries on as if he had never called on Us when harm first touched him."** [*Yūnus* (10): 12], **"Any blessing you have is from Allāh. Then when harm touches you, it is to Him you cry for help. But when He removes the harm from you, a group of you associate others with their Lord, ungrateful for what We have given them."** [*al-Naḥl* (16): 53-55], **"When harm occurs to you at sea, those you call on vanish - except for Him alone! But when He delivers you to dry land, you turn away. Man is truly ungrateful."** [*al-Isrā'* (17): 67], **"When harm touches man he calls upon his Lord, repenting to Him. Then when He grants him a blessing from Him, he forgets what he was calling for before and ascribes rivals to Allāh, so as to misguide others from His Way."** [*al-Zumar* (39): 8]

benefit, causing or repressing harm, granting and withholding, that only what He has decreed and determined will happen, and that the whole of creation is physically incapable of causing any harm or benefit reaching a person that has not already been ordained in the Book.

Actualising this, realising this leads the servant to sever any dependency he may have on creatures, it stops him asking of them, seeking their help and placing his hope in them to grant him benefit or repress harm.[8] It also stops him fearing them thinking that they will cause him benefit or harm. This, in turn, necessitates his singling out Allāh alone for obedience and worship. He will place obedience to Allāh at the fore, before obedience to creation. He will do his utmost to guard against His displeasure even if it means that, in the pursuit of this, he displease the whole of creation. A ḥadīth reported on the authority of Abū Saʿīd has the Messenger of Allāh (ﷺ) saying, "From the weakness of certainty is that a person please people by displeasing Allāh, that he praise them for provision that Allāh has granted him, and that he censure them for something that Allāh has with-

---

[8] Ḥalīmī, *al-Minhāj fī Shuʿab al-Īmān,* said, 'Hope takes on a number of forms: 1) hoping to attain what is desired 2) hoping to keep it after it has been attained 3) hoping to keep at bay all that is disliked and that it not occur 4) hoping to see the end of anything that is disliked that has already occurred. When the feeling of hope becomes deeply ingrained in a person, it leads to state of submissiveness and humility in the same way that this state is achieved when fear takes firm root in the heart. This is because hope and fear go hand in hand, the one who is in a state of fear hopes for the opposite of what he fears - He supplicates to Allāh and asks of Him; likewise the one in state of hope fears losing what he desires and hence takes refuge with Allāh from this and asks of Him. Hence there is no one who is in a state of fear except that he too is in a state of hope and vice-versa.'

held from him. The avarice of a person will not grant the provision of Allāh and neither will the aversion of anyone avert it."[9]

Fine indeed are the words of the poet:

Would that you could take relish when life is bitter
Would that you could be content when creatures are angry
If you have true love, everything becomes easy
For everything above the earth is mere dust.

Know that every creature walking on the earth is merely dust. How then can a person place obeying such a creature before the Lord of lords? How can one please dust by displeasing the King, the Bestower? This is truly perplexing!

In many places, the Qur'ān lays the foundation to the tenant that Allāh, Glorious is He, alone is the one who gives and withholds:

---

[9] Abū Nu'aym, *al-Ḥilyah*, vol. 5, pg. 106, Bayhaqī, *Shu'ab* #207 who said that the isnād contains Muḥammad ibn Marwān who is ḍa'īf. Dhahabī, *al-Mīzān*, vol. 4, pg. 32 said, 'They have abandoned him and some of them accused him of lying.' The isnād also contains 'Aṭiyyah al-'Awfī who is ḍa'īf. Suyūṭī, *al-Jāmi'* #2493 ruled it ḍa'īf and Albānī, *al-Ḍa'īfah* #1482 ruled it mawḍū'.

Ṭabarānī, *al-Kabīr* #10514 and Bayhaqī #208 record on the authority of ibn Mas'ūd that the Prophet (ﷺ) said, "Do not please anyone by displeasing Allāh, do not praise anyone for Allāh's grace, do not censure anyone for something that Allāh did not want (to happen). The avarice of a person will not grant the provision of Allāh and neither will the aversion of anyone avert it." It was ruled mawḍū' by Albānī, *Ḍa'īf al-Targhīb* #1064

Bayhaqī #209 and ibn Abī al-Dunyā, *al-Yaqīn* #32 record a similar wording as a statement of ibn Mas'ūd. cf. Chapter nine fn. 29

مَّا يَفْتَحِ ٱللَّهُ لِلنَّاسِ مِن رَّحْمَةٍ فَلَا مُمْسِكَ لَهَا ۖ
وَمَا يُمْسِكْ فَلَا مُرْسِلَ لَهُۥ مِنۢ بَعْدِهِۦ ۚ

"Any mercy Allāh opens up to people, no one can withhold, and any He withholds, no one can afterwards release."[10]

وَإِن يَمْسَسْكَ ٱللَّهُ بِضُرٍّ فَلَا كَاشِفَ لَهُۥٓ إِلَّا هُوَ ۖ وَإِن
يُرِدْكَ بِخَيْرٍ فَلَا رَآدَّ لِفَضْلِهِۦ ۚ

"If Allāh afflicts you with harm, no one can remove it except Him. If He desires good for you, no one can avert His favour."[11]

قُلْ أَفَرَءَيْتُم مَّا تَدْعُونَ
مِن دُونِ ٱللَّهِ إِنْ أَرَادَنِىَ ٱللَّهُ بِضُرٍّ هَلْ هُنَّ كَـٰشِفَـٰتُ ضُرِّهِۦٓ
أَوْ أَرَادَنِى بِرَحْمَةٍ هَلْ هُنَّ مُمْسِكَـٰتُ رَحْمَتِهِۦ ۚ قُلْ حَسْبِىَ
ٱللَّهُ ۖ عَلَيْهِ يَتَوَكَّلُ ٱلْمُتَوَكِّلُونَ ﴿٣٨﴾

"Say: 'So what do you think? If Allāh desires harm for me, can those you call upon besides Allāh remove His harm? Or if He desires mercy for me, can they withhold His mercy?' Say: 'Allāh is enough for me. All those who truly trust put their trust in Him.'"[12]

---

[10] *Fāṭir* (35): 2

[11] *Yūnus* (10): 107

[12] *al-Zumar* (39): 38

He, Most High, relates from His Prophet, Nūḥ (*'alayhis-salām*),

يَٰقَوْمِ إِن كَانَ كَبُرَ عَلَيْكُم
مَّقَامِى وَتَذْكِيرِى بِـَٔايَٰتِ ٱللَّهِ فَعَلَى ٱللَّهِ تَوَكَّلْتُ فَأَجْمِعُوٓا۟
أَمْرَكُمْ وَشُرَكَآءَكُمْ ثُمَّ لَا يَكُنْ أَمْرُكُمْ عَلَيْكُمْ غُمَّةً ثُمَّ ٱقْضُوٓا۟
إِلَىَّ وَلَا تُنظِرُونِ ﴿٧١﴾

"My people, if my standing here and reminding you of Allāh's signs has become too much for you to bear, know that I have put my trust in Allāh. So decide, you and your gods on what you want to do and be open about it..."[13]

He, Most High, relates from His Prophet, Hūd (*'alayhis-salām*),

إِنِّىٓ أُشْهِدُ ٱللَّهَ
وَٱشْهَدُوٓا۟ أَنِّى بَرِىٓءٌ مِّمَّا تُشْرِكُونَ ﴿٥٤﴾ مِن دُونِهِۦ فَكِيدُونِى
جَمِيعًا ثُمَّ لَا تُنظِرُونِ ﴿٥٥﴾ إِنِّى تَوَكَّلْتُ عَلَى ٱللَّهِ رَبِّى وَرَبِّكُم

"I call on Allāh to be my witness, and you also bear witness, that I am free of all the gods you have apart from Him. So scheme against me, all of you together, and then grant me no respite. I have put my trust in Allāh, my Lord and your Lord..."[14]

One of them said,

---

[13] *Yūnus* (10): 71

[14] *Hūd* (11): 54-56

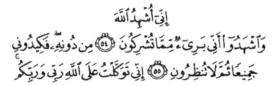

Anything Allāh has decreed for me must occur
Who can avert the decree through circumspection?
Allāh is more deserving of us than our own selves
What are we save subjects, governed by His decree?

A man once complained to Fuḍayl al-Fāqah to which he responded, 'Is it another besides Allāh that you want to govern your affairs?'

One of them said,

Govern! Your governance will not avail
The decree will pass over all you administer
The Lord regulates all affairs
Everything He ordains, the decrees take after.

CHAPTER NINE

The Virtues of Patience

The Messenger of Allāh (ﷺ) said, "Know that great good lies in bearing with patience what you dislike." The narration of 'Umar, the freed-slave of Ghufrah, on the authority of ibn 'Abbās has an additional sentence before this phrase, "If you are able to work deeds for the sake of Allāh, being content and in a state of certainty, do so. If you are unable, know that great good lies in bearing with patience what you dislike."[1]

The meaning of certainty here is to actualise faith in the decree. This is mentioned explicitly in the narration of his son, 'Alī ibn 'Abdullāh ibn 'Abbās, on the authority of his father which has the additional wording, 'I asked, 'Messenger of Allāh, how can I act with certainty?' He replied, "That you know that what afflicted you could never have missed you and what missed you could never have afflicted you."' However, the isnād is ḍa'īf.

When you have consolidated the topic of certainty, attaining certainty in the heart of the decree and ordainment necessitates the heart being at rest and peace with it. This very meaning is

---

[1] Abū Nu'aym, vol. 1, pg. 314

articulated by the Qur'ān:

مَآأَصَابَ
مِن مُّصِيبَةٍ فِى ٱلْأَرْضِ وَلَا فِىٓ أَنفُسِكُمْ إِلَّا فِى كِتَـٰبٍ
مِّن قَبْلِ أَن نَّبْرَأَهَآ ۚ إِنَّ ذَٰلِكَ عَلَى ٱللَّهِ يَسِيرٌ ﴿٢٢﴾

"Nothing occurs, either in the earth or in your selves, without its being in a Book before We make it happen. That is so that you will not be grieved about the things that pass you by or exult about the things that come to you."[2]

In exegesis to this verse, Ḍaḥḥāk said, 'He strengthened their resolve: *"so that you will not be grieved about the things that passed you by,"* so grieve not about worldly effects (that have missed you), for We have not decreed them for you. *"Or exult about the things that come to you,"* exult not about the worldly effects that We have granted you for they would never have been held back from you.' This was recorded by ibn Abī al-Dunyā.

Sa'īd ibn Jubayr explained the verse with the words, '*"So that you will not be grieved about the things that passed you by,"* of well-being and affluence, this because you know that it was decreed for you before He even created you.' This was recorded by ibn Abī Ḥātim.

It is in light of this that one of the Salaf said, 'Faith in the decree removes worry and distress.' The Prophet (ﷺ) alluded to this with his words, "Be desirous of all that would benefit you and seek Allāh's aid and do not despair. If you are afflicted with something, do not say, 'If only I had done [this], such and such

---

[2] *al-Ḥadīd* (57): 22-23

would have happened,' rather say, 'Allāh decreed and did what He willed.' [Saying], 'If only,' opens [the door to] the actions of Shayṭān."[3]

Alluded to in this ḥadīth is that if one were to, at the onset of affliction, remind one's self of the decree, the whisperings of Shayṭān which lead to worry, distress and sorrow would go away.

Anas said, 'I served the Prophet (ﷺ) for ten years and he never once said to me about something I did, "Why did you do that?" or about something I did not do, "Why didn't you do that?"'[4] He said, 'When one of his family would reprimand me, he would say, "Let him be, if something is decreed, it will happen."' The ḥadīth with this additional wording was recorded by Imām Aḥmad.[5]

Ibn Abī al-Dunyā records with an isnād that is problematic that 'Ā'ishah said, 'The most frequent words of the Prophet (ﷺ) when he came home were, "Whatever matter Allāh has ordained will happen."' He also records, with an isnād that is mursal, that the Prophet (ﷺ) said to ibn Mas'ūd, "Do not worry too much, what has been decreed will happen, and what you are to be provided with will come to you."[6] The ḥadīth of Abū Hurayrah has the

[3] Muslim #2664 on the authority of Abū Hurayrah.

[4] Bukhārī #2768-6038-6911, Muslim #2309

[5] Aḥmad #13418, Bayhaqī, *Shu'ab* #8070 with an isnād meeting the criteria of Bukhārī and Muslim.
cf. Arna'uṭ, *Takhrīj Musnad.*

[6] Bayhaqī, *Shu'ab* #1188, Ibn Abī al-Dunyā, *al-Faraj ba'd al-Shiddah.*

=

Prophet (ﷺ) saying, "[Saying], '*Lā ḥawla wa lā quwwata illā bi'llāh*'[7] is a cure for ninety nine ailments, the least of which is worry." This was recorded by Ṭabarānī and Ḥākim.[8]

Actualising this statement necessarily leads to relegating all affairs to Allāh and believing that nothing will happen unless Allāh wills it. Faith in this removes worry and distress. The Prophet (ﷺ) advised a man, saying, "Do not impugn Allāh for something He has ordained for you."[9]

When the servant sees the workings of Allāh's wisdom and mercy through His decree and ordainment and knows that He is not to be impugned for His decree, he will attain contentment at Allāh's ordainment. Allāh, Mighty and Magnificent, says,

---

=

Ibn Ḥajr, *al-Iṣābah*, vol. 1, pg. 104 said that the isnād contained 'Ayyāsh ibn 'Abbās who was ḍa'īf. It was ruled ḍa'īf by Albānī, *al-Ḍa'īfah* #4793. cf. Albānī, *al-Ṣaḥīḥah* vol. 4, pg. 34 who mentions two more weak narrations of this ḥadīth on the authority of 'Umar and Abū Dharr.

[7] lit: There is no might nor motion except with Allāh.

[8] Ṭabarānī, *al-Awsaṭ* #5028, Ibn Abī al-Dunyā, *al-Faraj ba'd al-Shiddah*.
Ḥākim #1990 said it was ṣaḥīḥ but Dhahabī pointed out that it had a weak narrator, Bishr. Haythamī, vol. 10, pg. 98 said the isnād contained Bishr ibn Rāfi' who was ḍa'īf. Ibn al-Jawzī, *al-'Ilal*, vol. 2, pg. 348 said that it was not authentic and it was ruled ḍa'īf by Albānī, *Ḍa'īf al-Targhīb* #970-1147

[9] Aḥmad #17814-22717, Bukhārī, *Khalq Af'āl al-'Ibād* #163
Mundhirī, *al-Targhīb* vol. 2, pg. 257, after quoting two chains, said of one of them that the isnād was ḥasan. It was ruled ḥasan li ghayrihī by Albānī, *al-Ṣaḥīḥah* #3334, *Ṣaḥīḥ al-Targhīb* #1307. Arna'ūt said that the ḥadīth was a candidate for being ḥasan.

مَآ أَصَابَ مِن
مُّصِيبَةٍ إِلَّا بِإِذْنِ ٱللَّهِ ۗ وَمَن يُؤْمِنۢ بِٱللَّهِ يَهْدِ قَلْبَهُۥ

"No misfortune occurs except by Allāh's permission. Whoever has faith in Allāh - He will guide his heart."[10]

In exegesis to this verse, 'Alqamah said, 'This refers to a misfortune that befalls a person, but he knows that it is from Allāh so he accepts it and is content.'

In an authentic ḥadīth, the Prophet (ﷺ) said, "There is nothing that Allāh ordains for the believer except that it is good for him. If he encounters times of ease, he is grateful and that is good for him. If he encounters misfortune, he is patient and that is good for him. This only holds true for the believer."[11]

The Qur'ān also proves this,

قُل لَّن يُصِيبَنَآ إِلَّا مَا كَتَبَ
ٱللَّهُ لَنَا هُوَ مَوْلَىٰنَا ۚ وَعَلَى ٱللَّهِ فَلْيَتَوَكَّلِ ٱلْمُؤْمِنُونَ
﴿٥١﴾ قُلْ هَلْ تَرَبَّصُونَ بِنَآ إِلَّآ إِحْدَى ٱلْحُسْنَيَيْنِ

"Say: 'Nothing can happen to us except what Allāh has ordained for us. He is our Master and it is in Allāh that the believers should put their trust.' Say: 'What do you await for us except for one of

[10] *al-Taghābun* (64): 11

[11] Muslim #2999 on the authority of Ṣuhayb ibn Sinān

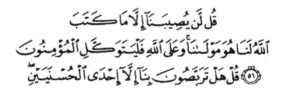

the two best things?...'"[12]

Here, He informs us that nothing could happen to them except what He has decreed. This indicates that, regardless if what they encounter is hard or easy, it is the same to them. He then informs us that He is their Master and whoever is in such a position will not be forsaken by Allāh; indeed He will take charge of effectuating good for him,

فَٱعْلَمُوٓا۟ أَنَّ ٱللَّهَ مَوْلَىٰكُمْ ۚ نِعْمَ ٱلْمَوْلَىٰ وَنِعْمَ ٱلنَّصِيرُ

"Know that Allāh is your Master, the Best of Masters and the Best of Helpers!"[13]

هَلْ تَرَبَّصُونَ بِنَآ إِلَّآ إِحْدَى ٱلْحُسْنَيَيْنِ

"What do you await for us except for one of the two best things?..."[14]

i.e. either aid and victory or martyrdom: both are best.[15]

Tirmidhī records on the authority of Anas that the Prophet (ﷺ) said, "When Allāh loves a people, He tries them. Whoever is content will have good-pleasure, and whoever is displeased will

[12] *al-Tawbah* (9): 51-52

[13] *al-Anfāl* (8): 40

[14] *al-Tawbah* (9): 52

[15] Ibn Abī Ḥātim and Ṭabarī quote this as the exegesis of ibn 'Abbās and Mujāhid.

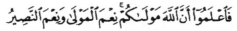

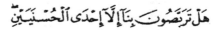

have displeasure."[16]

Abū'l-Dardā' said, 'Allāh loves that a [servant] be content with a matter when He ordains it.' Ummu'l-Dardā' said, 'Those who are truly content with the ordainment of Allāh are people who are content, no matter what is ordained. On the Day of Rising they will have such stations in Paradise as would make the martyrs envious.'

Ibn Mas'ūd said, 'By Allāh's justice and knowledge did He place relief and joy in certainty and contentment, and worry and distress in doubt and displeasure.' This is also reported as a ḥadīth of the Prophet (ﷺ) but is ḍa'īf.[18]

'Umar ibn 'Abdu'l-'Azīz would say, 'These invocations have left me with no further needs, only submission to the decree of Allāh, Mighty and Magnificent. He would employ them in supplication frequently, saying, "O Allāh make me content with your ordainment and bless me in your decree to the extent that I would not wish to hasten something I delayed or delay something I

---

[16] Tirmidhī #2396, ibn Mājah #4031.

Tirmidhī said that it was ḥasan gharīb. Mundhirī, *al-Targhīb*, vol. 4, pg. 233 said the isnād was ḥasan or ṣaḥīḥ. Ibn Mufliḥ, *al-Ādāb al-Shar'iyyah*, vol. 2, pg. 181 said that the isnād was jayyid. It was ruled ḥasan by Albānī, *al-Ṣaḥīḥah* #146

Aḥmad #23623-23633-23641 records a similar ḥadīth on the authority of Maḥmūd ibn Labīd with the words, "When Allāh loves a people, He tries them. Whoever is patient, for him is patience and whoever despairs, for him is despair." Arna'ūṭ said that the isnād was jayyid.

[17] Bayhaqī, *Shu'ab* #209, ibn Abī al-Dunyā, *al-Yaqīn* #32 with a ḍa'īf isnād.

[18] cf. Chapter 8 fn #8

hastened.'"[19]

Ibn 'Awn said, 'In both times of ease and difficulty be content with Allāh's decree, it will decrease your distress and serve you better in your pursuit of the Hereafter. Know that the servant will never attain the reality of contentment until his contentment at times of poverty and tribulation is the same as his contentment at times of affluence and ease. How can you go to Allāh to adjudge your affair and then be discontent when you find that His ordainment does not accord to your desires?! It is well possible that, were your desire to come to fruition, you would be destroyed! When His ordainment accords to your desires, you are content, and both cases arise because of your scant knowledge of the unseen. How can you go to Him for judgment when this is your condition! You have not been fair to yourself and neither have you hit the mark with regards to contentment.'

These are fine words. The meaning is that when the servant turns to Allāh, Mighty and Magnificent, to aid him in a decision (*istikhāra*), he should be content with what Allāh chooses for him regardless if it conforms to his desires or not. This is because he, himself, does not know in which course the good lies and Allāh, Glorious is He, is not to be impugned for His ordainment. It is for this reason that some of the Salaf, such as ibn Mas'ūd[20] and others, would order a person who feared that he would not be able to bear a decision which opposed his desires, to add the words, 'in all well-being,' to his *istikhāra* since He could choose trial for him and he not be able to bear it. This has also been

[19] Bayhaqī, *Shu'ab* #227

[20] Bayhaqī, *Shu'ab* #205

recorded from the Prophet (ﷺ) but it is ḍaʿīf.[21]

Bakr al-Muzanī narrates that a man would frequently make *istikhāra* and as result was tried and was unable to bear it with patience, instead sinking into despair. So Allāh revealed to one of their Prophets, "Tell My servant that if he lacks due resolve then why does he not ask for My decision [with the words], 'in all well-being'?"

The ḥadīth of Saʿd has the Prophet (ﷺ) saying, "From the good fortune of a servant is His seeking a decision from his Lord, Mighty and Magnificent, and being content with what He ordains. From the misery of a person is his abandoning seeking a decision and his dislike of what He ordains." This was recorded by Tirmidhī and others.[22]

There are numerous ways to achieve contentment with the decree:

1. The servant having certainty in Allāh and a firm trust that whatever He decrees for a believer will be good for him. As such he will be like a patient who has submitted to the ministrations of a skilled doctor: such a patient will be content with his ministrations be they painful or not because he has a complete trust that the doctor is doing only that which will be of benefit to him.

---

[21] Ṭabarānī, *al-Kabīr* #10012-10052 on the authority of ibn Masʿūd and it is ḍaʿīf.

[22] Aḥmad #1445, Tirmidhī #2151
Tirmidhī said that it was gharīb and that its isnād contained Ḥammād ibn Ḥumayd who was not strong. Arnaʿūṭ said that the isnād was ḍaʿīf. It was ruled ḍaʿīf by Albānī, *al-Ḍaʿīfah* #1906

This is what ibn 'Awn alluded to in his aforementioned words.

2. Looking to the reward that Allāh has promised for contentment. The servant could well be so engrossed in pondering this that he forgets all about the pain he is facing. It is reported that a righteous woman from the Salaf tripped and broke a nail whereupon she laughed saying, 'The delight of His reward has made me forget the bitterness of His pain.'

3. Immersing oneself in love of the One who sends tribulation, constantly being aware of His magnificence, beauty, greatness and perfection which is without limit. The potency of such awareness will cause the servant to drown in it such that he no longer senses pain much in the same way that the women who saw Yūsuf forgot about the pain of cutting their hands.[23] This is a higher station than those previously mentioned.

Junaid said that he asked Sirrī if the lover senses the pain of tribulation to which he replied, 'No.' In these words, he is alluding to this station. It is in this light that a group of those facing tribulation said, 'Let Him do what He wills with us. Even if He were to cut us up, limb by limb, we would only increase in our love.'

One of them said,

> If ardent love tore me apart, limb from limb,
> The pain would only increase me in love.

---

[23] Mentioned in, "**When they saw him, they were amazed by him and cut their hands. They said, 'Allāh preserve us! This is no man. What can this be but a noble angel here!'**" [*Yūsuf* (12): 31]

I will remain a prisoner to love,
Until, in the pursuit of your pleasure, I pass away.

Ibrāhīm ibn Adham left his wealth, property, children and servants. While performing *ṭawāf*, he saw his son but did not speak to him. He said,

I migrated from all people for love of You.
I bereaved my dependants that I may see You.
If You tore my limbs apart, in my love
The heart would still long for You.

A group of the lovers such as Fuḍayl and Fatḥ al-Mawṣilī, if they went to sleep without an evening meal and without a lamp being lit, they would cry in joy.

During the winter nights, Fatḥ would gather his family and cover them with his cloak and say, 'You made me go hungry so I have made my family go hungry. You have made me a stranger so I have made my family strangers. This You do with Your beloved and Your friends, am I one of them? Should I exult in joy?'[24]

They entered upon one of the Salaf who was ill and asked him, 'Is there anything you want?' He replied, 'That whatever He finds most pleasing, I find most pleasing.'[25]

In this light, one of them said,

---

[24] Abū Nu'aym, vol. 8, pg. 192

[25] Dhahabī, *Siyar*, vol. 9, pg. 182 quoting it from Yaḥya ibn Sa'īd al-Qaṭṭān.

For Your sake, his punishment is sweet.
For Your sake, his distance is closeness.
You are like my very soul,
Rather, You are more beloved!
Sufficient is it in my love
That I love only what You love.

Abū'l-Turāb composed the following lines:

Be not deceived, the lover has signs.
He has routes to the gifts of the Beloved:
Taking delight at the bitterness of His trial,
Being joyous at all that He does,
His withholding is a gift accepted,
Poverty is honour and generosity, transient.

They entered upon a man whose son had been martyred in Jihād and he wept saying, 'I do not cry at his loss, I only cry when thinking what his state of contentment with Allāh was when the swords struck!'

If Ghaḍā's people wish me dead, so be it
By Allāh, I have never begrudged the beloved's wish!
I am like a slave to them: I cannot object.

The point here is that the Prophet (ﷺ) enjoined ibn 'Abbās to work deeds while in state of contentment if he was able to. If not, he said, "If you are unable, know that great good lies in bearing with patience what you dislike," this then proves that being content with decrees that are hard to bear is not an obligation but rather a recommendation, a state of excellence. Whoever is unable to be content must instead be patient. Patience is obligatory, it must be present, and it contains great good. Allāh,

Most High, has commanded patience and promised a great reward for it:

إِنَّمَا يُوَفَّى ٱلصَّٰبِرُونَ أَجْرَهُم بِغَيْرِ حِسَابٍ ﴿١٠﴾

"The patient will be paid their wages in full without any reckoning."[26]

وَبَشِّرِ ٱلصَّٰبِرِينَ
﴿١٥٥﴾ ٱلَّذِينَ إِذَآ أَصَٰبَتْهُم مُّصِيبَةٌ قَالُوٓا۟ إِنَّا لِلَّهِ وَإِنَّآ إِلَيْهِ رَٰجِعُونَ
﴿١٥٦﴾ أُو۟لَٰٓئِكَ عَلَيْهِمْ صَلَوَٰتٌ مِّن رَّبِّهِمْ وَرَحْمَةٌ وَأُو۟لَٰٓئِكَ
هُمُ ٱلْمُهْتَدُونَ ﴿١٥٧﴾

"Give good news to the patient: those who, when disaster strikes them, say, 'We belong to Allāh and to Him we will return.' Those are the people who will have blessings and mercy from their Lord; they are the ones who are guided."[27]

وَبَشِّرِ ٱلْمُخْبِتِينَ ﴿٣٤﴾
ٱلَّذِينَ إِذَا ذُكِرَ ٱللَّهُ وَجِلَتْ قُلُوبُهُمْ وَٱلصَّٰبِرِينَ عَلَىٰ مَآ أَصَابَهُمْ

"Give good news to the humble hearted, whose hearts quake at the mention of Allāh, and who are patient in the face of all that happens to them."[28]

---

[26] *al-Zumar* (39): 10

[27] *al-Baqarah* (2): 155-157

[28] *al-Ḥajj* (22): 34-35

al-Ḥasan said, 'The state of contentment is rare, but patience is the recourse of the believer.'[29] Sulaymān al-Khawāṣ said, 'The station of patience is below that of contentment. Contentment is that a person, before the onset of tribulation, is content whether it is present or not. Patience is that a person, after the onset of tribulation, bears it steadfastly.'

The difference between patience and contentment is that patience is to restrain the soul and to prevent it from displeasure while sensing discomfort or pain.[30] Contentment necessitates that the heart readily accept what it is facing and, even if it was to feel some pain at what it is facing, the sense of contentment will lessen it, perhaps even remove it altogether. This is because the

---

[29] Abū Nu'aym, vol. 5, pg. 342 from 'Umar ibn 'Abdu'l-'Azīz

[30] *Ṣabr*: to refrain and withhold. Rāghib said, 'It is to withhold the soul as determined by the Legal Law and the intellect.' Jāḥiẓ said that it is a quality made up of sobriety and courage and Munāwī said that it was the ability to face disturbing and painful circumstances, both physical and mental. It is to withhold the soul from misery and displeasure, the tongue from complaining and the limbs from derangement; it is to remain firm upon the laws of Allāh in all circumstances and to face adversity with the best of conduct.

Ibn Ḥibbān, *Rawḍatu'l-'Uqalā'*, pp. 126-128, said, 'It is obligatory upon the intelligent, in the beginning, to adhere firmly to *ṣabr* at the onset of difficulty and when he becomes firm in this he should then move on to the level of contentment (*riḍā*). If one has not been nourished with *ṣabr* he should adhere firmly to inculcating *ṣabr* in himself (*taṣabbur*) for that is the first stages of *riḍā*. If a man was to have *ṣabr*, truly would he be noble; for *ṣabr* is the fount of all good and the foundation of all obedience... The stages leading to it are concern (*ihtimām*), awakening (*tayakkuẓ*), examination and circumspection (*tathabbut*), and *taṣabbur*, after it comes *riḍā* and that is the peak of the spiritual stations... *ṣabr* is displayed in three matters: *ṣabr* from sin; *ṣabr* upon obedience; and *ṣabr* in the face of adversity and calamity.' cf. Ibn al-Qayyim, *Madārij al-Sālikīn*, vol. 1, pp. 162-165

heart has felt the soothing breath of certainty and cognisance.[31]

This is why a large group of the Salaf such as 'Umar ibn 'Abdu'l-'Azīz, Fuḍayl, Abū Sulaymān and ibn al-Mubārak would say, 'The person who is content does not desire a state other than the one he is in whereas the patient does.' This state of being is reported from a group of the Companions, amongst whom were 'Umar and ibn Mas'ūd.

'Abdu'l-'Azīz ibn Abū Ruwwād said, 'Amongst the Children of Israel there was a devout worshipper who saw a dream in which he was told that so-and-so would be his wife in Paradise. So he went to her as a guest for three nights to see what she did. She would sleep while he prayed by night and she would eat while he fasted. When he left her, he asked her about the greatest deed she felt she did. She replied, "I do no more than what you have seen except that I have one quality: If I am in trying times, I do not want to be in times of ease. If I am ill, I do not wish to be healthy. If I am hungry, I do not wish to be full. And if I am in the sun, I do not wish to be in the shade." He said, "By Allāh, this is a quality that is beyond the reach of the servants!"'

---

[31] *Riḍā*: the opposite of displeasure and malcontent. Jurjānī said that it referred to the joy of the heart at the occurrence of the decree. Ibn al-Qayyim, *Madārij*, vol. 2, pg. 185 mentioned that it is the tranquillity of the heart in the face of the vicissitudes of the decree and the firm knowledge that it has that Allāh would only that which is good for it.

Bayhaqī, *Shu'ab* #209 records that ibn Mas'ūd (*raḍiyAllāhu 'anhu*) said, '*Riḍā* is that you not please the people at the expense of the displeasure of Allāh; that you not praise anyone for the provision Allāh has granted you; and that you not blame anyone for that which Allāh has not given you. The grant of provision is not dictated by the avarice of a person and neither is it withheld because of the aversion of another. By Allāh's justice and knowledge did He place relief and joy in certainty and contentment, and worry and distress in doubt and displeasure.'

Patience is to be shown at the onset of calamity as is authentically reported from the Prophet (ﷺ).[32] Contentment is shown after the onset of calamity as the Prophet (ﷺ) said in his supplication, "I ask You for contentment after the decree."[33] This is because a servant could well resolve to be content at the decree before it occurs, but the resolve dissipate when he actually faces it. Whoever is content after the decree has befallen is one who is truly content.[34]

Therefore, in summary, patience is obligatory and must be present. Beyond patience there is displeasure and malcontent and whoever is displeased at the decree of Allāh, his lot will be displeasure. Moreover, the pain he will face and the malice of his enemies will be far greater than his despair, just as one of them said,

Despair not at any mishap that befalls
Allow not the malice of the enemy free hold
People, through patience will you see your hopes
When you meet the opposing army, stand firm!

The Prophet (ﷺ) said, "Whoever inculcates patience in himself, Allāh will grant him patience. Allāh has not granted anyone a gift better and more expansive than patience."[35]

---

[32] Bukhārī #1283-1302-7154, Muslim #626 on the authority of Anas

[33] Aḥmad #18325, Nasā'ī #1306-1307 on the authority of 'Ammār ibn Yāsir It was ruled ṣaḥīḥ by ibn Ḥibbān #1971, Ḥakim #1923 with Dhahabī agreeing, Albānī, *Takhrīj al-Nasā'ī* and Arna'ūṭ.

[34] cf. Khaṭṭābī, *Sha'n al-Du'ā*, pg. 132

[35] Bukhārī #1469-6470, Muslim #1053 on the authority of Abū Sa'īd al-Khudrī

'Umar said, 'The best times of our lives have been those accompanied by patience.'[36] 'Alī said, 'Patience with respect to faith is like the head with respect to the body: a person who has no patience has no faith.'[37]

al-Ḥasan said, 'Patience is one of the treasures of Paradise. Allāh only confers it to those He ennobles.' Maymūn ibn Mihrān said, 'No Prophet or anyone else has ever attained good except through patience.' Ibrāhīm al-Taymī said, 'Allāh does not gift a servant with patience at harm, patience at tribulation and patience at calamity except that He has conferred on him the best [gift] after faith in Allāh, Mighty and Magnificent.' He derived this from the saying of Allāh, Most High,

﴿لَّيْسَ ٱلْبِرَّ أَن تُوَلُّوا۟ وُجُوهَكُمْ قِبَلَ ٱلْمَشْرِقِ وَٱلْمَغْرِبِ وَلَٰكِنَّ
ٱلْبِرَّ مَنْ ءَامَنَ بِٱللَّهِ وَٱلْيَوْمِ ٱلْءَاخِرِ وَٱلْمَلَٰٓئِكَةِ وَٱلْكِتَٰبِ
وَٱلنَّبِيِّـۧنَ وَءَاتَى ٱلْمَالَ عَلَىٰ حُبِّهِۦ ذَوِى ٱلْقُرْبَىٰ وَٱلْيَتَٰمَىٰ
وَٱلْمَسَٰكِينَ وَٱبْنَ ٱلسَّبِيلِ وَٱلسَّآئِلِينَ وَفِى ٱلرِّقَابِ وَأَقَامَ
ٱلصَّلَوٰةَ وَءَاتَى ٱلزَّكَوٰةَ وَٱلْمُوفُونَ بِعَهْدِهِمْ إِذَا عَٰهَدُوا۟
وَٱلصَّٰبِرِينَ فِى ٱلْبَأْسَآءِ وَٱلضَّرَّآءِ وَحِينَ ٱلْبَأْسِ ۗ أُو۟لَٰٓئِكَ ٱلَّذِينَ
صَدَقُوا۟ ۖ وَأُو۟لَٰٓئِكَ هُمُ ٱلْمُتَّقُونَ ﴿١٧٧﴾

[36] Bukhārī as a ta'līq report. Ibn Ḥajr, *Fatḥ*, vol. 11, pg. 309, said, 'Aḥmad, *Kitāb al-Zuhd* (#117), provided a complete chain to Mujāhid who said that "Umar said...' and it is ṣaḥīḥ.' It is also recorded by ibn al-Mubārak, *al-Zuhd* #630, Wakī', *al-Zuhd* #198

[37] Ibn Abī Shaybah, *al-Īmān* #130, Wakī' #199, Bayhaqī, *Shu'ab* #40, Abū Nu'aym, vol. 1, pp. 75-76
Suyūṭī, *al-Jāmi'* #5136 ruled it ḍa'īf.

> **"...rather, those with true devoutness are those who have faith in Allāh and the Last Day, the Angels, the Book and the Prophets, and who, despite their love for it, give away their wealth to their relatives and to orphans and the very poor, and to travellers and beggars and to set slaves free, and who establish prayer and pay zakāt; those who honour their contracts when they make them, and are patient in poverty and illness and in battle. Those are the people who are true. They are the people who have *taqwā*."**[38]

'Umar ibn 'Abdu'l-'Azīz said, 'Allāh does not grant a blessing to a person only to take it away, leaving patience in its place, except that the replacement was better than what was removed.' Then he recited,

إِنَّمَا يُوَفَّى ٱلصَّٰبِرُونَ أَجْرَهُم بِغَيْرِ حِسَابٍ ﴿١٠﴾

> **"The patient will be paid their wages in full without any reckoning."**[39]

One of the righteous would have a piece of paper which he kept in his pocket. Every hour he would look at it and read it. Written therein were the words,

وَٱصْبِرْ لِحُكْمِ رَبِّكَ فَإِنَّكَ بِأَعْيُنِنَا

> **"So wait patiently for the judgement of your Lord**

[38] *al-Baqarah* (2): 177

[39] *al-Zumar* (39): 10

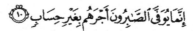

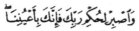

- you are certainly before Our eyes."[40]

Beautiful patience is a servant's keeping his tribulation to himself and not telling anyone about it. Allāh, Most High says,

فَصَبْرٌ جَمِيلٌ

"But beauty lies in patience."[41]

In exegesis to this, a group of the Salaf said that it referred to patience that was not accompanied by any form of complaint.[42]

Aḥnaf ibn Qays had lost his sight for forty years, yet he told no one. 'Abdu'l-'Azīz ibn Abū Ruwwād became blind in one eye for twenty years, then, one day, his son looked at him carefully and said, 'Father, one of your eyes is blind!' He replied, "Yes my son, for the past twenty years have I been content with Allāh." Imām Aḥmad would never complain of any illness that afflicted him to anyone. It was mentioned to him that Mujāhid would dislike moaning while ill, so he stopped doing it and never did so till the day he died. He would exhort his self saying, 'Be patient or you will regret!'

One of the Gnostics visited a sick person who was saying, 'Ah! Ah!' He asked, 'Who from?' One of them said,

---

[40] *al-Ṭūr* (52): 48

[41] *Yūsuf* (12): 83

[42] cf. Ṭabarī.
Refer to Appendix 2 for a further discussion on patience by ibn al-Qayyim.

The soul is beset with illness
Yet it hides its malady from those who visit
The inner self has not been just if it complains
Of its desires to other than its beloved

Yaḥyā ibn Mu'ādh said, 'If you love your Lord and He decreed hunger and nakedness for you, it would be obligatory for you to bear it and withhold it from creation. The lover patiently bears harm from his beloved, so why would you present your complaints to it for something it has not done to you?'

In my view, deeds from any
besides You are hateful.
You do acts and they,
coming from You, are beautiful.

The Messenger of Allāh (ﷺ) and his Companions would tie rocks to their bellies against the hunger they faced.[43]

Uwais would collect broken pieces of bone from the rubbish heap with dogs crowding around him trying to do the same. One day a dog barked at him and he said, 'Dog, do not harm one who does not harm you, eat what is close to you and I will eat what is close to me. If I enter Paradise, I would be better than you, and if I enter the Fire, you would be better than me.'

Ibrāhīm ibn Adham would collect ears of grain along with the poor. Seeing that they disliked his competing with them in acquiring them, he thought, 'I have abandoned property at Balkh to compete with the poor in collecting grain?' After that he would

[43] Bukhārī #6452 on the authority of Abū Hurayrah

only ever gather grain amongst the animals who would pasture in that land.

Imām Aḥmad would collect grain with the poor. Sufyān al-Thawrī was once employed to look after two camels while on the road to Mecca. He cooked food for some people and it tasted so bad that they beat him for it. Fatḥ al-Mawṣilī would build fires for people for a wage.

For Your sake did I leave the land
To the malicious, to the envious.
Master, for how long will I remain in Your good grace
My life rushes by, my need is not fulfilled.

Another said,

Much subjugation and toil
have I seen pursuing Your grace.
Much patience have I born for You
in the face of illness and frailty.
Abandon me not,
I cannot do without You.
If you wish a wage,
take my soul.
For Your good pleasure
I have born ardent love.
My heart is deeply in love,
my tears choke me.
The love of You makes
all that I face easy to bear.
A person does not sense blessing
if he has not faced hardship.

In their view, the tribulations of this world would be blessings. One of them said, 'The true jurist is one who sees tribulation as a blessing and ease a misfortune.' It is mentioned in a Judaeo-Christian narration, 'If you see someone affluent approaching, say, "A sin whose punishment has been hastened on!" If you see someone poor approaching, say, "A sign of the righteous, welcome!"'[44]

One of the Salaf said, 'When I am afflicted with calamity, I praise Allāh four times: I praise Allāh for it not being worse than it is, I praise Allāh for nourishing me with the ability to bear it patiently, I praise Him for granting me the accord to say, "To Allāh we belong and to Him we return," and I praise Him for not making the tribulation in my religion.'

Looking to relief through patience is an act of worship since tribulation never remains forever.

Patiently bear every calamity, take heart,
Know that harm never endures forever.
Be patient, just as the nobles were patient:
It is a fleeting event; here today, gone tomorrow.

If the most severely afflicted person were to be dipped but once in the bliss of Paradise and then asked, 'Have you ever seen calamity? Have you ever encountered calamity?' He will reply, 'My Lord, no!'[45]

---

[44] This was said by Shurayḥ al-Qāḍī as per Dhahabī, *Siyar*, vol. 4, pg. 105

[45] As mentioned in a ḥadīth recorded by Muslim #2807 on the authority of Anas.

O soul, patience only for a few days!
Their length? A few flitting dreams!
O soul, pass through this world quickly;
Turn away from it, true life lies ahead!

Another said,

It is only an hour, then it will depart
All of this will go, it will disappear.

CHAPTER TEN

Patience and Victory

The Messenger of Allāh (ﷺ) said, "and that victory comes with patience." This statement is in full accord with the sayings of Allāh, Most High,

يَٰٓأَيُّهَا ٱلَّذِينَ ءَامَنُوٓاْ إِذَا لَقِيتُمْ فِئَةً
فَٱثْبُتُواْ وَٱذْكُرُواْ ٱللَّهَ كَثِيرًا لَّعَلَّكُمْ تُفْلِحُونَ ﴿٤٥﴾

"You who have faith! When you meet a troop, stand firm and remember Allāh repeatedly so that hopefully you will be successful."[1]

إِن يَكُن مِّنكُمْ عِشْرُونَ صَٰبِرُونَ
يَغْلِبُواْ مِاْئَتَيْنِ ۚ وَإِن يَكُن مِّنكُم مِّاْئَةٌ يَغْلِبُوٓاْ أَلْفًا مِّنَ
ٱلَّذِينَ كَفَرُواْ

"If there are twenty of you who are patient, they will overcome two hundred; and if there are a hundred of you, they will overcome a thousand

[1] *al-Anfāl* (8): 45

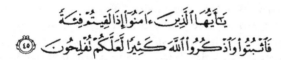

of those who disbelieve."[2]

He said, concerning the story of Ṭālūt,

فَلَمَّا جَاوَزَهُۥ هُوَ وَٱلَّذِينَ ءَامَنُوا۟ مَعَهُۥ قَالُوا۟
لَا طَاقَةَ لَنَا ٱلْيَوْمَ بِجَالُوتَ وَجُنُودِهِۦ ۚ قَالَ ٱلَّذِينَ
يَظُنُّونَ أَنَّهُم مُّلَـٰقُوا۟ ٱللَّهِ كَم مِّن فِئَةٍ قَلِيلَةٍ
غَلَبَتْ فِئَةً كَثِيرَةًۢ بِإِذْنِ ٱللَّهِ ۗ وَٱللَّهُ مَعَ ٱلصَّـٰبِرِينَ ﴿٢٤٩﴾

"Then when he and those who had faith with him had crossed it, they said, 'We do not have the strength to face Goliath and his troops today.' But those who were sure that they were going to meet Allāh said, 'How many a small force has triumphed over a much greater one by Allāh's permission! Allāh is with the patient.'"[3]

Allāh, Most High, says,

بَلَىٰٓ ۚ إِن تَصْبِرُوا۟ وَتَتَّقُوا۟ وَيَأْتُوكُم مِّن فَوْرِهِمْ
هَـٰذَا يُمْدِدْكُمْ رَبُّكُم بِخَمْسَةِ ءَالَـٰفٍ مِّنَ ٱلْمَلَـٰٓئِكَةِ مُسَوِّمِينَ

"Yes indeed! But if you are patient and have *taqwā* and they come upon you suddenly, your Lord will reinforce you with five thousand angels clearly identified."[4]

---

[2] *al-Anfāl* (8): 65

[3] *al-Baqarah* (2): 249

[4] *Āli 'Imrān* (3): 125

there are many more verses and aḥādīth concerning being patient when meeting the enemy.

'Umar asked the elders of Banū 'Abasa, 'What tool do you fight people with?' They replied, 'With patience. We have never fought a people except that we were patient and steadfast like they were patient and steadfast.'

One of the Salaf said, 'All of us dislike death and the pain of injury, however we attain varying degrees through patience.'

Baṭṭāl was asked about courage to which he replied, 'Patience for an hour.'

All this pertains to fighting the external enemy: fighting the disbelievers, but the same applies to fighting the internal enemy: fighting the lower self and base desires. Indeed, fighting these is one of the greatest forms of Jihād. The Prophet (ﷺ) said, "The Mujāhid is one who strives against his soul for the sake of Allāh."[5]

'Abdullāh ibn 'Amr replied to a person who asked about Jihād by saying, 'Start with your self and strive against it. Start with your self and start a campaign against it!'

It is reported on the authority of Jābir, with a ḍa'īf isnād, that

---

[5] Aḥmad #23951, Tirmidhī #1261 on the authority of Faḍālah.

Aḥmad #23957 with the words, "...upon the obedience of Allāh," with a ṣaḥīḥ isnād. Aḥmad #23965 with the words, "...in the Way of Allāh," with a ṣaḥīḥ isnād. Tirmidhī #1621 with the words, "The Mujāhid is one who strives against his soul," and he said it was ḥasan ṣaḥīḥ.

Tirmidhī said it was ḥasan ṣaḥīḥ and it was ruled ṣaḥīḥ by ibn Ḥibbān #6424, Ḥakim #24, Albānī, *al-Ṣaḥīḥah* #549 and Arna'ūṭ.

the Prophet (ﷺ) said to a people who had returned from battle, "You have returned from the lesser Jihād to the greater Jihād." It was asked, 'What is the greater Jihād?' He replied, "The servant's striving against his base desires."[6]

When Abū Bakr al-Ṣiddīq appointed 'Umar (*raḍiyAllāhu 'anhu*) as *Khalīfah*, he advised him, 'The first thing you have to beware of is your self inside of you.'

It is reported in the ḥadīth of Sa'd ibn Sinān on the authority of Anas (*raḍiyAllāhu 'anhu*), and in the mursal ḥadīth of Mālik al-Ashja'ī, that the Prophet (ﷺ) said, "Your enemy is not that person who, if he kills you, guarantees your entry in Paradise, or if you kill him, he will be a light for you. Your worst enemy is your self inside you."[7]

The poet, 'Abbās ibn al-Aḥnaf encapsulated this meaning in a poem,

My heart calls me to what will harm me,

---

[6] Bayhaqī, *al-Zuhd al-Kabīr* #373 and he said that the isnād contains weakness.

It was ruled ḍa'īf by ibn Rajab as above and in *Jāmi' al-'Ulūm*, vol. 1, pg. 489. Ibn Taymiyyah, *Majmū' al-Fatāwā*, vol. 11, pg. 197 said that it had no basis and in *al-Mustadrak 'ala al-Majmū'*, vol. 1, pg. 221 that it is not authentic. Zayla'ī, *Takhrīj al-Kashshāf*, vol. 2, pg. 395 said that it was gharīb jiddan. Ibn Ḥajr, *al-Kāfī*, pg. 194 said, 'It contains 'Īsā ibn Ibrāhīm from Yaḥyā ibn Ya'lā from Layth ibn Abū Sulaym all of whom are ḍa'īf.' Albānī, *al-Ḍa'īfah* #2460 ruled it munkar.

'Alī al-Qārī, *al-Asrār al-Marfū'ah* #211 quoted ibn Hajr stating that it is a saying of Ibrāhīm ibn Abū 'Ablah and the author, *Jāmi' al-'Ulūm*, vol. 1, pg. 489 also quotes it as his saying.

[7] Ṭabarānī, *al-Kabīr* #3445 from Abū Mālik al-Ash'arī and it was ruled ḍa'īf by Albānī, *Ḍa'īf al-Targhīb* #1890

Increasing my sorrow and my pain.
How can I guard against my enemy,
When the enemy resides inside me?

This Jihād also requires patience, whoever steadfastly strives against his self, his desires and his shayṭān will achieve victory. Whoever, on the other hand, despairs and gives up patience will be overcome, defeated and imprisoned. He will become subjugated and mean, imprisoned by his shayṭān and his desires. It is said,

If a person does not defeat his desires
They will render the noble, ignoble

Another said,

Perhaps a stranger is imprisoned by passion,
Yet in the face of patience it dissipates.
A person beset with lusts is a slave,
But if he subdues them, he is a king!

Ibn al-Mubārak said, 'Whoever is patient will end up finding little requiring patience. Whoever despairs will find little to take pleasure in.'

Bukhārī and Muslim record that the Prophet (ﷺ) said, "The strong person is not a person who wrestles, but the strong person is that person who can control his self when angry."[8]

A person described Aḥnaf ibn Qays with the words, 'He had a

[8] Bukhārī #6114, Muslim #2608 on the authority of Abū Hurayrah.

complete mastery over his self when angry.' A person remarked to one of them, 'So-and-so can walk on water.' He replied, 'If Allāh grants a person the ability to oppose his desires, such a one is stronger than the person who can walk on water.'

Know that your self is like an animal, if it knows that you are firm and resolute, it will not waver, but if it knows that you are lazy and irresolute, it will take advantage and hanker after its wants and pursue its lusts.

Abū Sulaymān al-Dārānī would say, 'While in Iraq, I was in charge of [up keeping] the palaces, the vessels, clothes and food of the princes and my soul did not want any of them. Then I was put in charge of dates and my soul almost fell upon them.' This was mentioned to one of the Gnostics who said, 'He had no hope of attaining the first so his lusts did not hanker after them, but he did want the second, so they did hanker after them.'

> Steadfastly I avoided delights
> till they vanished.
> I forced my soul to forego them,
> They remained absent.
> The soul goes where
> A person directs.
> If it sees an opportunity,
> It hankers after it, otherwise not,
> For many a day my self
> Gained ascendancy.
> Yet when it saw my resolve
> At humility, it submitted.

Therefore, his saying, *"and that victory comes with patience,"* subsumes patience and steadfastness in striving against both the external and internal enemy. The Salaf would view this latter patience: patiently striving against the self and desires to be better than patience in the face of tribulation.

Maymūn ibn Mihrān said, 'Patience is of two categories: patience when encountering calamity which is good, and patience in avoiding sins which is better.' Sa'īd ibn Jubayr said, 'Patience is of two types: the best form is patience in avoiding what Allāh has proscribed and doing those acts of worship that He has made obligatory, and patience when facing calamity.'

A ḥadīth having this meaning is reported from the Prophet (ﷺ) on the authority of 'Alī but it is not authentic.[9]

[9] Ibn Abī al-Dunyā, *al-Ṣabr* #24 with the words, "Patience is of three types: patience when encountering calamity, patience in obedience, and patience in avoiding sin..."

CHAPTER ELEVEN

Relief Accompanies Distress

The Messenger of Allāh (ﷺ) said, "and that relief comes with distress." This is proven by the sayings of Allāh, Most High,

وَهُوَ ٱلَّذِى يُنَزِّلُ ٱلْغَيْثَ مِنۢ بَعْدِ مَا قَنَطُوا۟ وَيَنشُرُ رَحْمَتَهُۥ ۚ
وَهُوَ ٱلْوَلِىُّ ٱلْحَمِيدُ ﴿٢٨﴾

"It is He who sends down abundant rain, after they have lost all hope, and unfolds His mercy. He is the Protector, the Praiseworthy."[1]

ٱللَّهُ ٱلَّذِى يُرْسِلُ ٱلرِّيَٰحَ فَتُثِيرُ سَحَابًا فَيَبْسُطُهُۥ
فِى ٱلسَّمَآءِ كَيْفَ يَشَآءُ وَيَجْعَلُهُۥ كِسَفًا فَتَرَى ٱلْوَدْقَ يَخْرُجُ مِنْ
خِلَٰلِهِۦ ۖ فَإِذَآ أَصَابَ بِهِۦ مَن يَشَآءُ مِنْ عِبَادِهِۦٓ إِذَا هُمْ يَسْتَبْشِرُونَ
﴿٤٨﴾ وَإِن كَانُوا۟ مِن قَبْلِ أَن يُنَزَّلَ عَلَيْهِم مِّن قَبْلِهِۦ لَمُبْلِسِينَ

"It is Allāh who sends the winds which stir up clouds which He spreads about the sky however He wills. He forms them into dark clumps and

---

[1] *al-Shūrā* (42): 28

> **you see the rain come pouring out from the middle of them. When He makes it fall on those of His servants He wills, they rejoice, even though before He sent it down on them they were in despair."[2]**

In a ḥadīth reported by Abū Razīn al-'Uqaylī, the Prophet (ﷺ), "Our Lord laughs at the despair of His servant when His altering of his circumstances is imminent."[3] This was recorded by Imām Aḥmad. His son, 'Abdullāh, also records a lengthy ḥadīth on the authority of Abū Razīn that the Prophet (ﷺ) said, "On the day that (He will) send rain, Allāh knows that He will see you in a state of despair and He will laugh knowing that the change He will bring about is imminent."[4]

The meaning is that Allāh, Glorious is He, is amazed at the despondency of His servants, their fear, their misgivings and their giving up hope of His mercy when He has decreed that their circumstances are soon to change, while they remain unaware, and rain is to fall.

While the Prophet (ﷺ) was standing, delivering the Friday ser-

---

[2] *al-Rūm* (30): 48-49

[3] Aḥmad #16187-16201, ibn Mājah #181, 'Abdullāh ibn Aḥmad, *al-Sunnah* #452-453

Ibn Taymiyyah, *al-Wāsiṭiyyah*, said that the ḥadīth was ḥasan. Suyūṭi, *al-Jāmi'* #5207 said it was ṣaḥīḥ. Arna'ūṭ said that the isnād was ḍa'īf as did Albānī, *al-Ṣaḥīḥah* #2810 but he ruled the ḥadīth ḥasan due to supporting witnesses.

[4] Aḥmad #16206, 'Abdullāh ibn Aḥmad, *al-Sunnah* #452-453, Ṭabarānī, *al-Kabir*, vol. 19, pg. 211 #477

The isnād is ḍa'īf. cf. Albānī, *al-Ṣaḥīḥah* #2810 and Arna'ūṭ.

mon, a man came to him complaining of drought and the straitened circumstances everyone was in. The Prophet (ﷺ) raised his hands and supplicated for rain whereupon rain clouds gathered and it rained continuously till the following Friday when they asked him (ﷺ) to supplicate for the rain to stop. He did so and the skies cleared.[5]

In His Book, Allāh has narrated numerous stories that deal with relief coming after distress and hardship. He told us of His rescuing Nuḥ and those with him on the ark from the *"terrible plight"*[6] wherein the earth's population were all drowned. He informed us of His saving Ibrāhīm (*'alayhis-salām*) from the fire kindled by the polytheists and how He made it *"coolness and peace"*[7] for him. He also narrated to us how He ordered Ibrāhīm to slaughter his son and, at the last moment, how He ransomed him with a *"mighty sacrifice."*[8] He told us of the story of Mūsā and how his mother placed him in the river and his subsequently being found by Pharaoh's family. He informed us of the story of Mūsā and Pharaoh: how He saved Mūsā and drowned his enemy. He narrated the story of Ayyūb, Yūnus, Ya'qūb, Yūsuf and the story of Yūnus's people when they believed. He also told us about numerous incidents in the life of Muḥammad (ﷺ) where He came to his aid and saved him such as when he was in the cave, at the Battle of Badr, the Battle of Uḥud and the Battle of Ḥunayn.

[5] Bukhārī #932-933-1013-1019-1021-1029-1033-3582-6093-6342, Muslim #897 on the authority of Anas.

[6] *al-Anbiyā'* (21): 76

[7] *al-Anbiyā'* (21): 69

[8] *al-Ṣāffāt* (37): 107

He told us the story of 'Ā'ishah when she was falsely accused and how He absolved her of that accusation.[9] He narrated to us the story of the three

وَعَلَى ٱلثَّلَٰثَةِ ٱلَّذِينَ خُلِّفُواْ حَتَّىٰٓ إِذَا ضَاقَتْ عَلَيْهِمُ ٱلْأَرْضُ بِمَا رَحُبَتْ وَضَاقَتْ عَلَيْهِمْ أَنفُسُهُمْ وَظَنُّوٓاْ أَن لَّا مَلْجَأَ مِنَ ٱللَّهِ إِلَّآ إِلَيْهِ ثُمَّ تَابَ عَلَيْهِمْ لِيَتُوبُوٓاْ

> **"who were left behind, so that when the earth became narrow for them, for all its great breadth, and their own selves became constricted for them and they realised that there was no refuge from Allāh except in Him, He turned to them so that they might turn to Him."**[10]

The Sunnah mentions many such incidents such as the story of the three who were trapped in the cave by a falling boulder and they supplicated to Allāh, making mention of their righteous deeds, and He relieved them.[11] And such as the story of Ibrāhīm and Sārah with the tyrant who coveted her for his own ends and

---

[9] The full story is recorded by Bukhārī #2661-4141-4690-4750-4757-6679-7369-7370-7500-7545 and Muslim #2770 on the authority of 'Ā'ishah.

[10] *al-Tawbah* (9): 118
The full story is recorded by Bukhārī #2757-2947-2950-3088-3556-3889-3951-4417-4673-4676-4677-4678-6255-6690-7225 and Muslim #2769 on the authority of Ka'b ibn Mālik.

[11] Bukhārī #2215-2272-2333-3465-5974 and Muslim #2743 on the authority of ibn 'Umar

how Allāh defeated the evil plot.[12]

Such events occurring to Muslims and those before Islām are too many to mention, many of them are collated in books such as ibn Abī al-Dunyā's *al-Faraj ba'd al-Shiddah* and *Mujābī al-Du'ā* and in the book *al-Mustaghīthīn bi'llāh wa'l-Mustaṣrikhīna bihi*, and the books dealing with the miracles of the *Awliyā'*, the biographies of the righteous and the works of history.

One of the scholars - I think he was from Morocco - mentioned in a book of his that he heard Abū Dharr al-Harawī, the Ḥāfiẓ, narrate that, while he was in Baghdād reading to Abū Ḥafṣ ibn Shāhīn in a perfume sellers shop, he saw a man coming to the perfume seller and giving him ten dirhams in return for whatever he needed, he placed the items in a bowl and put the bowl on his head. He slipped and his bowl fell, breaking all the items and he began to cry profusely saying, 'In a caravan I lost a camel carrying four hundred - or he said four thousand - dīnārs and with them stones for rings which were worth even more. However, I do not despair at their loss but I have just had a son born to me and we need the items that a woman needs after having given birth and all I had were these ten dirhams! Then, when what was decreed just happened, I fell into despair. I have nothing to give them tonight and no work tomorrow that I may bring something home, the only thing I can think of is to run away and let them die in peace.' Abū Dharr said, 'An elder from al-Jund, sitting at the threshold of his house, heard the story and he sought Abū Ḥafṣ's permission to enter his house along with his colleagues while the afflicted person was yet with him. He granted them

[12] Bukhārī #2217-2635-3357-3358-5084-6950 and Muslim #2371 on the authority of Abū Hurayrah.

permission and the elder asked the man to repeat his story and asked him who was in the caravan he spoke of and where he lost the camel. He told him and was asked, "If you saw it, would you recognise it?" He replied, "Yes." The man brought out the camel and when he saw it he said, "That's it," and he described the stones it carried. When its baggage was opened, they saw those stones in it, so the elder returned it to him and he became wealthy once again. When the man had left, the Jundi man wept and when asked why, he said, "The only wish I had left in this world was that Allāh bring the owner of this wealth to me to retrieve it. Now that Allāh has fulfilled that wish by His grace, I have no further wish left to meet and so I know that the time of death is near.'" Abū Dharr said, 'He passed away less than a month later and we prayed over him, may Allāh have mercy on him.'

The same author narrated from someone in Mawsul that there was a trader there who would travel to different lands to ply his trade. One time he travelled to Kūfah with all of his trade goods and everything he owned. During this journey he met a person who served him well, they became fast friends and he came to trust him completely. Then, while they had stopped at a rest station, he took advantage of him and stole all his property and provisions, leaving him with nothing. He searched and searched but was unable to find out where the servant had gone so, on foot and starving, he returned to his land. He entered his city by night and knocked on his door. When his family learned it was him, they rejoiced and praised Allāh for his return saying, 'Your wife has just given birth to a son and we have no money to buy the things a woman needs post-delivery. Tonight, we are very hungry so buy some flour and oil for the lamps.' When he heard this, his misery and distress increased. Unwilling to tell them what had happened, he left to a nearby shop and extended the salām to the shopkeeper and gathered the oil and everything else he needed. Then, while talking to him, he saw his saddlebag lying unguarded on the ground in the shop and asked how it got there. The shopkeeper said, 'A man bought food from me and asked me to host him. I put his saddle-bag in my shop and tied his beast in my neighbour's house. The man is sleeping in the Masjid.' Taking the saddle-bag with him, he went to the Masjid to find the man sleeping. He kicked him and he awoke alarmed. 'Thief! Betrayer! Where is my wealth?' he cried. He replied, 'It is in the bag around your neck,' and when he looked he found that nothing was missing at all. He then retrieved his beast, spent lavishly on his family and then told them all that had happened.

A similar story is related by Tinnawkhī, *al-Faraj ba'd al-Shiddah*. It is lengthy, but in summary: At the time of al-Rashīd there lived a money-exchanger who bought a slave-girl for five hundred dīnārs. He fell deeply in love her, and in wanting to be with her all the time, his business suffered immensely. He spent all his capital and was left with nothing. The slave-girl became pregnant and he began to take his house apart and sell the effects therein until nothing remained, then, while in this state, she went into labour and asked him to buy what she needed for birth and post-birth complaining that she would die if he did not hurry. Weeping, he immediately left the house having resolved to drown himself in the Tigris. He was about to jump in, when the fear of Allāh struck him and stopped him; instead he travelled on foot from city to city until he reached Khurasān where he stopped and commenced employment. He wrote sixty six letters to his home town asking after the slave-girl but got no response and determined that she had indeed passed away. Many years later he decided to return to Baghdād and took with him his property to the value of twenty thousand ḍīnārs. The caravan was attacked by highway robbers and they stole everything leaving him, once again, poor and needy. He continued on his journey until he reached Baghdād, entering it in the same state that he had left it some thirty years ago. He went to his house to find it well looked after with a beautiful entrance, there were doorkeepers, servants and mules. He asked who lived in the house and he was told that it belonged to such-a-such money-changer, the name they gave was his name and they said that the mother was foster mother to the Leader of the Believer's son and that the owner of the house himself was in charge of the Bayt al-Māl. The person he had asked told him that his father had told him that the father of this money-changer also used to be a successful money-changer who, being beset with poverty, left seeking items for the mother when she was in labour and had lost his way and died. His mother had begged help from some neighbours who came to her assistance. Then, the Leader of the Believers had a son born to him, Ma'mūn, and he would accept the milk of no foster mother save hers; so, while in his service, she came to hold a position of respect and honour in his household. 'Then, when Ma'mūn became Khalīfah, he kept the woman and her son with him and her son built this house you see,' he finished. The man asked if the mother was still alive and he replied, 'Yes, she spends some days with the Khalīfah and some days with her son.' The money-changer, the son, arrived with a group of people and entered his house; the man went in as well. The son fulfilled their needs and they left, leaving the man alone. The youth asked, 'Old man, what is it you need?' He replied, 'I am your father.' His face went white and he quickly jumped up and led the man into his house, sitting him on a chair. There was a screened area in the room and the old man remarked. 'Perhaps you should ask so-and-so if I am telling the truth,' mentioning his mothers name. The mother, the slave-girl, heard his voice and raised the screens and rushed to her master, kissing him and weeping. He informed them of his story and they took him to al-Ma'mūn who had him take his son's position and promoted the son.

Ibn Abī al-Dunyā, *al-Faraj ba'd al-Shiddah*, records with his isnād to Waḍḍāḥ ibn Khaythama who said, "Umar ibn 'Abdu'l-'Azīz, may Allāh have mercy on him, ordered me to release all the prisoners in a prison, so I released them all save Yazīd ibn Abī Muslim who vowed to have my blood in revenge. I was in Africa when I was told that Yazīd ibn Abī Muslim, recently appointed Amīr of the African provinces, had arrived. I fled. He sent people after me who caught me and took me to him. He said, "By Allāh, I have been asking Him repeatedly to allow me to find a way to you!" He said, "By Allāh, I have been asking Him repeatedly to save me from your evil!" He said, "By Allāh, He has not granted you safety and I will kill you! Were the Angel of Death itself to race me in taking away your soul, I would beat it! Bring a sword and the executioners mat!" I was made to kneel on it and shackled, the executioner stood over me, sword ready. Then the call to prayer was given and he went to pray, when he went into prostration, an army attacked him, killing him. A man came and cut me free and told me to go on my way.'

He also records, with his isnād to 'Umar al-Sarāyā who was, one time, fighting in the Roman provinces by himself. Once, while sleeping, one of them came to him and prodded him with his foot, awaking him. 'O Arab,' he said, 'you have a choice: I can kill you with a spear, a sword or we can wrestle!' He said, 'Then, let us wrestle.' He beat me and, sitting on my chest, asked, 'How should I kill you?' I cried out, 'I bear witness that everything that is worshipped beneath your Throne is false save Your noble face. You see my circumstances so save me!' I then fell in a swoon and when I came to, I found the Roman lying dead besides me.

Abū'l-Ḥasan ibn al-Jahḍam records with his isnād to Ḥātim al-Aṣamm who said, 'We encountered the Turks and had a jousting match. A Turk threw me off my horse and then dismounted and sat on my chest. Grabbing my beard, he took a knife out of his sock and moved to slaughter me. My heart, however, was not with him or his knife, it was with my Master. I thought, "My Master, if You have decreed my slaughter here, I fully submit to Your ordinance. I belong to You." While in that situation, one of the Muslims shot him with an arrow and he fell off me. I stood up and, taking his knife from his hand, slaughtered him with it.'

Let your hearts reside with your Master and you will see such wonders of His providence unfurl that were never seen by your predecessors!

There are many more incidents such as these but what we have mentioned thus far is enough.

CHAPTER TWELVE

Ease Accompanies Hardship

The Messenger of Allāh (ﷺ) said, "and that with hardship comes ease." This statement is taken from His, Glorious is He, sayings,

سَيَجْعَلُ ٱللَّهُ بَعْدَ عُسْرٍ يُسْرًا ۝٧

"Allāh will appoint after difficulty, ease."[1]

فَإِنَّ مَعَ ٱلْعُسْرِ يُسْرًا ۝٥ إِنَّ مَعَ ٱلْعُسْرِ يُسْرًا ۝٦

"For truly with hardship comes ease; truly with hardship comes ease."[2]

Ḥumayd ibn Ḥammād ibn Abū al-Khuwār narrated that 'Ā'idh ibn Shuraiḥ narrated to him that he heard Anas ibn Mālik saying, 'The Prophet (ﷺ) was sitting in front of a hole in the ground and remarked, "If hardship were to enter this burrow, ease would follow it in and remove it." Then Allāh revealed,

---

[1] *al-Ṭalāq* (65): 7

[2] *al-Sharḥ* (94): 5-6

فَإِنَّ مَعَ ٱلْعُسْرِ يُسْرًا ۝٥ إِنَّ مَعَ ٱلْعُسْرِ يُسْرًا ۝٦

"For truly with hardship comes ease; truly with hardship comes ease."[3]

This was recorded by ibn Abī Ḥātim, *al-Tafsīr* and it was recorded by Bazzār with the wording, "'Were hardship to come and enter this burrow, ease would follow it in and remove it. Then He recited, *"For truly with hardship comes ease."*

They have ruled Ḥumayd ibn Ḥammād ḍa'īf.[4] Ibn Jarīr records on the authority of Ma'mar from al-Ḥasan who said, 'The Prophet (ﷺ) came out one day, joyous and happy, saying, "One hardship will never overcome two eases."'"[5]

---

[3] *al-Sharḥ* (94): 5-6

[4] Ibn Abī Ḥātim #19395, Bazzār #2288, Ṭabarānī, *al-Awsaṭ* #3416

It was also recorded by Ḥākim #3010 and Dhahabī said, 'It was singularly narrated by Ḥumayd ibn Ḥammād on the authority of 'Ā'idh and both are munkar in their narration of ḥadīth.' Bayhaqī, *Shu'ab* #10012 said that it was ḍa'īf and Albānī, *al-Ḍa'īfah* #1403 said that it was ḍa'īf jiddan.

[5] Ṭabarī, Bayhaqī, *Shu'ab* #10013, Ḥākim #3950 and Dhahabī said it was mursal as did Zayla'ī, *Takhrīj al-Kashshāf*, vol. 4, pg. 235. Ibn Ḥajr, *al-Kāfī*, pg. 319 said that it was mursal and that the mawṣūl version was ḍa'īf, in *Taghlīq al-Ta'līq*, vol. 4, pg. 372 he adds that the isnād to al-Ḥasan is ṣaḥīḥ. Albānī, *al-Ḍa'īfah* #4342 said that it was ḍa'īf.

Ibn Abī Ḥātim #19396 records it as a saying of al-Ḥasan.

Ibn Kathīr said, 'The meaning of these words is that in both occurrences, the word *difficulty* is appended to the definite article, *al*, as such it is singular. The word *ease* is left indefinite; as such there is more than one occurrence of it. Therefore the second reference to *difficulty* denotes the same as in the first reference, whereas there is more than one instance of *ease*.'

فَإِنَّ مَعَ ٱلْعُسْرِ يُسْرًا ﴿٥﴾ إِنَّ مَعَ ٱلْعُسْرِ يُسْرًا ﴿٦﴾

"For truly with hardship comes ease; truly with hardship comes ease."[6]

He also records this via the route of 'Awf and Yūnus from al-Ḥasan as a mursal ḥadīth. He also records it as a ḥadīth of Qatādah who said, 'It has been mentioned to us that the Messenger of Allāh (ﷺ) gave his Companions the glad-tidings of this verse saying, "One hardship will never overcome two eases."'[7]

Ibn Abī al-Dunyā records the ḥadīth of Mu'āwiyah ibn Qurrah on the authority of someone who narrated to him that ibn Mas'ūd said, 'Were hardship to enter a burrow, ease would follow it in.'[8] Then he recited,

فَإِنَّ مَعَ ٱلْعُسْرِ يُسْرًا ﴿٥﴾ إِنَّ مَعَ ٱلْعُسْرِ يُسْرًا ﴿٦﴾

"For truly with hardship comes ease; truly with hardship comes ease."[9]

He also records the ḥadīth of 'Abdu'l-Raḥmān ibn Zayd ibn Aslam from his father from his grandfather that when Abū 'Ubaydah was besieged, 'Umar wrote to him saying, 'No matter

---

[6] *al-Sharḥ* (94): 5-6

[7] Ṭabarī and it is mursal. Ibn Ḥajr, *Taghliq al-Ta'līq*, vol. 4, pg. 372 said that the isnād was ṣaḥīḥ up to Qatādah.

[8] Bayhaqī, *Shu'ab* #10011. Suyūṭī, *al-Durr* references it ibn Abī al-Dunyā, *al-Sabr* Ibn Ḥajr, *Taghlīq al-Ta'līq*, vol. 4, pg. 372 said that the isnād was jayyid.

[9] *al-Sharḥ* (94): 5-6

what hardship a person faces, Allāh will send relief afterwards for one hardship cannot overcome two eases and He says,

يَٰٓأَيُّهَا ٱلَّذِينَ ءَامَنُوا۟ ٱصْبِرُوا۟
وَصَابِرُوا۟ وَرَابِطُوا۟ وَٱتَّقُوا۟ ٱللَّهَ لَعَلَّكُمْ تُفْلِحُونَ ﴿٢٠٠﴾

> **"You who have faith! Be patient; be supreme in patience; be firm on the battlefield; and have *taqwā* of Allāh so that hopefully you will be successful."**[10, 11]

This was also how ibn 'Abbās[12] and other exegetes explained this verse saying, 'One hardship will never overcome two eases.'

While one of the early people was in the open desert in a state of extreme grief, a line of poetry came to him,

When a man awakes aggrieved,
I think death is better for him.

When night came, he heard a voice call out,

Be assured O person

---

[10] *Āli 'Imrān* (3): 200

[11] Ibn Abī al-Dunyā, *al-Faraj ba'd al-Shiddah*, pg. 24, Bayhaqī, *Shu'ab* #10010, ibn Abī Shaybah, vol. 5, pg. 335, vol. 13, pg. 37
Ḥākim #3176 said it was ṣaḥīḥ, meeting the criteria of Muslim, and Dhahabī agreed; however ibn Ḥajr, *Taghlīq al-Ta'līq*, vol. 4, pg. 372 said that the isnād was ḥasan.

[12] Sakhāwī, *al-Maqāṣid* #877 said, 'It was mentioned by al-Farrā' from al-Kalbī from Abū Ṣāliḥ.'

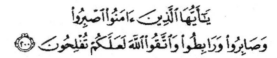

Beset with worry!
Poetry has he recited,
Still uppermost in his mind:
When hardship intensifies,
Ponder, *"Did We not expand..."*[13]
A hardship lies between two eases
When you recognise that, rejoice!

He said, 'I memorised these verses and Allāh relieved me of my distress.'

Many poems are written this vein; we shall select a few to quote here:

Be patient, patience yields wonders.
Despair not at calamity,
Ease closely follows adversity.
At hard times, adversity is removed.

One of them said:

Many are those who despair at events
The relief from which is imminent.

Another said,

Perhaps relief is soon to follow,
We treat our souls with 'perhaps'.
Closest is a person to relief
When he surrenders to despair.

---

[13] *al-Sharḥ* (94): 1

Another recited,

When affairs become hard, expect relief
Relief is imminent when adversity intensifies.

Another composed the following lines,

Despair not if you are aggrieved for a day,
You have been living in ease for many a day.
Do not think lowly of your Lord,
Beauty is most befitting for Him.
Do not relinquish hope; that is disbelief!
Allāh will make you suffice with little,
Know this: ease follows hardship,
Allāh is the most truthful of all who speak.

One of them said,

Patience is the key to relief's door.
Ease follows every hardship.
Time does not stagnate:
One event follows another.

We will conclude this treatise by mentioning some of the subtleties, benefits and wisdoms of tribulation:

1. The expiation of sins and being rewarded for bearing tribulation with patience. The scholars have differed if a person will be rewarded for the actual tribulation itself.

2. The servant is reminded of his sins so that he can repent and turn back to Allāh, Mighty and Magnificent.

3. The heart becomes soft after having been coarse and hard. One of the Salaf said, 'A person could fall ill and as a result bring his sins to mind. Then, by virtue of his fear of Allāh, they would break up and disperse like flies and Allāh would forgive him.'

4. A person humbling himself and submitting himself before Allāh, Mighty and Magnificent. Indeed such a state is more beloved to Allāh than many deeds of obedience.

5. They lead a person's heart to return to Allāh, to stand at His door, implore Him and to be submissive before Him. This is one of the greatest benefits of tribulation. Allāh has censured those who are not submissive to Him at times of hardship,

وَلَقَدْ أَخَذْنَٰهُم بِٱلْعَذَابِ فَمَا ٱسْتَكَانُوا۟ لِرَبِّهِمْ
وَمَا يَتَضَرَّعُونَ ﴿٧٦﴾

"We seized them with the punishment, but they did not go low before their Lord; nor will they humble themselves."[14]

وَلَقَدْ أَرْسَلْنَآ
إِلَىٰٓ أُمَمٍ مِّن قَبْلِكَ فَأَخَذْنَٰهُم بِٱلْبَأْسَآءِ وَٱلضَّرَّآءِ لَعَلَّهُمْ يَتَضَرَّعُونَ

"We sent Messengers to nations before you and afflicted their nations with hardship and distress so that hopefully they would humble themselves."[15]

---

[14] *al-Mu'minūn* (23): 76

[15] *al-An'ām* (6): 43

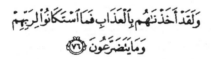

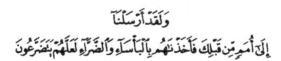

One of the previous Scriptures states, 'Allāh puts a servant to trial because He loves to hear his humble entreaty.'

Sa'īd ibn 'Abdu'l-'Azīz said, 'Dāwūd (*'alayhis-salām*) said, "Glory be to the One who causes a person to supplicate when faced with tribulation. Glory be to the One who confers gratitude to a person in a state of ease."'

Abū Ja'far Muḥammad ibn 'Alī passed by Muḥammad ibn al-Munkadir who was in state of intense grief. He asked after him and he was told that he was burdened by debt. Abū Ja'far said, 'Has the door of supplication opened for him?' They said, 'Yes.' He said, 'A servant is truly blessed if, when in need, he frequently invokes his Lord, no matter what that need.'

Some of them, when supplicating at times of adversity, would not want a quick response for fear that the state (of need of their Lord) that they found themselves in would end. Thābit said, 'When the believer invokes Allāh, Allāh entrusts Jibrīl to fulfil his need saying, "Do not hasten in meeting his need for I love to hear the voice of My believing servant."' This is reported as a ḥadīth of the Prophet (ﷺ) but all its routes are ḍa'īf.[16]

One of the Salaf saw the Lord of Might in a dream and said, 'My Lord, I have invoked You so much but without response!' He replied, 'I love to hear your voice.'

6. Tribulation leads the heart to relish the delight of patience and to be content. This is a station of immense rank and impor-

[16] Ṭabarānī, *al-Awsaṭ* #8442 on the authority of Jābir.
Haythamī, vol. 10, pg. 151 said, 'Its isnād contains Isḥāq ibn 'Abdullāh ibn Abū Farwa who is matrūk.'

tance; the excellence of which we have already alluded to.

7. Tribulation leads to a servant giving up dependency on the creation and leads him to turn to the Creator alone. Allāh has told us that the polytheist turns to Allāh sincerely when supplicating to Him at times of need, what then of the believer?!

8. Tribulation leads a person to actualise and live *Tawḥīḍ* in his heart and this is the most sublime of stations and noblest of rankings.[17]

One of the Judeao-Christian narrations mentions, 'Tribulations brings you and Me together. Well-being brings you and your self together.'

[17] Refer to Appendix 3 for a more complete list of the benefits of tribulation.

Conclusion

Generally speaking, when adversity intensifies and misfortune increases, relief is close. Allāh, Most High, says,

حَتَّىٰٓ
إِذَا ٱسْتَيْـَٔسَ ٱلرُّسُلُ وَظَنُّوٓا۟ أَنَّهُمْ قَدْ كُذِبُوا۟ جَآءَهُمْ
نَصْرُنَا فَنُجِّىَ مَن نَّشَآءُ

"Then when the Messengers despaired and thought themselves denied, Our help came to them, and those We willed were saved."[1]

مَّسَّتْهُمُ ٱلْبَأْسَآءُ وَٱلضَّرَّآءُ
وَزُلْزِلُوا۟ حَتَّىٰ يَقُولَ ٱلرَّسُولُ وَٱلَّذِينَ ءَامَنُوا۟ مَعَهُۥ مَتَىٰ نَصْرُ ٱللَّهِ ۗ
أَلَآ إِنَّ نَصْرَ ٱللَّهِ قَرِيبٌ ﴿٢١٤﴾

"Poverty and illness afflicted them and they were shaken to the point that the Prophet and those who had faith with him said, 'When is Allāh's help

[1] *Yūsuf* (12): 110

coming?' Be assured that Allāh's help is very near."[2]

He informs us that Ya'qūb (*'alayhis-salām*) never gave up hope of meeting Yūsuf and that he asked his brothers,

اذْهَبُوا فَتَحَسَّسُوا مِن يُوسُفَ وَأَخِيهِ وَلَا تَايْئَسُوا
مِن رَّوْحِ اللَّهِ

"Seek news of Yūsuf and his brother. Do not despair of solace from Allāh."[3]

and he said,

عَسَى اللَّهُ أَن يَأْتِيَنِي بِهِمْ جَمِيعًا

"...perhaps Allāh will bring them all together."[4]

A wonderful wisdom in attaching the onset of relief to intense distress is that in such circumstances a person gives up hope in any object of creation relieving him. Instead the person turns to Allāh and depends on Him alone. When a person severs hope in creation and places his dependency on Allāh, then will He respond and relieve him. *Tawakkul*, trust,[5] is to stop raising ones

[2] *al-Baqarah* (2): 214

[3] *Yūsuf* (12): 87

[4] *Yūsuf* (12): 83

[5] Bayhaqī, *Shu'ab*, vol. 2, pp. 99-100 records that 'Alī ibn Aḥmad was asked about *tawakkul* to which he replied, 'That you relinquish yourself from depending on =

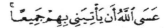

eyes to creation having given up hope in them. This was stated by Imām Aḥmad and he adduced as proof the saying of Ibrāhīm who, (when about to be burned in the fire), was asked by Jibrīl, 'Do you need anything?' He replied, 'From you, no.'[6]

Tawakkul is one of the greatest routes through which ones needs are met for Allāh suffices the person who puts his trust in Him,

وَمَن يَتَوَكَّلْ عَلَى ٱللَّهِ فَهُوَ حَسْبُهُۥٓ

"Whoever puts his trust in Allāh - He will be enough for him."[7]

Fuḍayl said, 'By Allāh! Were you to give up all hope in creation so that you no longer want anything from them, your Master would grant you everything you want!'

Another wisdom is that when hardship intensifies, the servant must strive against Shayṭān because he will whisper to him, caus-

=

your strength and ability, or the strength and ability of those like you.' Muḥammad ibn Sulayman said, '*Tawakkul* is that your heart never think that there is anyone who can bring you benefit or harm save Him; that you accept calmly everything that happens to you without aversion.'

[6] Bayhaqī, *Shu'ab* #1293 records from Abū Ya'qūb who said, 'The true reality of *tawakkul* was realised by Ibrāhīm the Khalīl of the All-Merciful, in that state in which he said to Jibrīl, "From you, no" because his soul was totally absorbed with Allāh and hence he no longer saw anything else besides Him, he was in a state of utter awe before Allāh, for the sake of Allāh. This is from the signs of *Tawḥīd* and Allāh manifesting His power for His Prophet, upon whom be peace.'

[7] *al-Ṭalāq* (65): 3

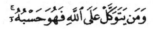

ing him to despair and give up hope. Man must repress these whisperings and the reward of striving against the enemy and repressing him will be the removal of the tribulation. The authentic ḥadīth mentions, "Your supplication will be answered so long as he is not impatient: he says, 'I have supplicated but have not received a response,' and therefore gives up supplication."[8]

Another wisdom is that if relief is slow in coming, and the servant gives up hope of ever receiving it, especially after a plenitude of supplication and humble entreaty, he will look inwards and blame his self saying, 'I have only been afflicted in this way because of you, if there was any good in you, I would have been answered.'

This self censure and realisation is more beloved to Allāh than many actions of obedience for it leads to a servant breaking his soul for the sake of his Master. The servant has acknowledged that he himself is not deserving of a response, and when in such a state, Allāh's response and relief is close at hand. Allāh is with those who have broken their souls for His sake, the extent of His mending is commensurate to the extent of the breaking.[9]

---

[8] Bukhārī #6340 and Muslim #2735 on the authority of Abū Hurayrah.

[9] The author, *al-Dhull wa'l-Inkisār*, writes, 'He, Glorious is He, is the mender of hearts that have broken for His sake. He, Glorious is He, comes close to hearts that are filled with humility to Him in the same way that He comes close to one who is standing in prayer, privately discoursing with Him. There is nothing that tends to the brokenness of the servant more than closeness and response.

Imām Aḥmad, may Allāh have mercy on him, records in his book, *al-Zuhd*, with his isnād to 'Imrān ibn al-Quṣayr who said, 'Mūsā ibn 'Imrān said, "My Lord, where should I seek You?" He replied, "Seek Me with those whose hearts have broken for My sake. Every day I come close to them by one arm-span and

=

Wahb said, 'A man worshipped Allāh for some time, then a need arose that he needed fulfilled so he fasted for seventy Saturdays, eating eleven dates every Saturday. He then asked Allāh for his need but it was not granted him so he looked to himself and said, "If there was any good in you, you would have been given your need!" At that point, an angel came down and said, "Son of Ādam, this hour which you are in is better for you than all your previous years of worship. Allāh has now fulfilled your need!"'

Whoever actualises this, knows this and witnesses this in his

=

were it not for this, they would surely perish."'

Ibrāhīm ibn al-Junaid, may Allāh have mercy on him, records in his book, al-Maḥabbah, with his isnād to Ja'far ibn Sulaymān who said, 'I heard Mālik ibn Dīnār saying, "Mūsā (*'alayhis-salām*) asked, 'My God, where should I seek You?' Allāh, Mighty and Magnificent, revealed to him, 'Mūsā, seek Me with those whose hearts have broken for My sake for I draw closer to them by an arm-span every day, and were it not for this, they would surely perish."' I asked Mālik ibn Dīnār, "What does broken hearts mean?" He replied, "I asked this question to one who rehearsed the scriptures and he said that he had asked this same question to 'Abdullāh ibn al-Sallām who replied, 'Broken hearts refers to those that have broken for the love of Allāh, Mighty and Magnificent, rather than the love of anything else.""'

The authentic Sunnah proves that Allāh is close to the heart that is broken by His tribulation, patient at His decree, and content. Muslim records on the authority of Abū Hurayrah that the Prophet (ﷺ) said, "Allāh, Might and Magnificent, will say on the Day of Rising, 'O son of Ādam, I was ill yet you did not visit Me.' He will say, 'My Lord, how could I visit You while You are the Lord of the worlds!' He will reply, 'Did you not know that such-and-such a servant of mine was ill yet you did not visit him? Did you not know that, were you to have visited him, you would have found Me with him?'"

Abū Nu'aym records via the route of Ḍamrah that ibn Shawdhab said, 'Allāh, Most High, revealed to Mūsā (*'alayhis-salām*), "Do you know why, from all people, I chose you for My message and speech?" He replied, "No, my Lord." He replied, "Because none was as modest and humble before Me as you were."'

heart will know that Allāh's blessings conferred in times of tribulation are greater than those bestowed in times of ease. This fact is reflected in the authentic ḥadīth in which the Prophet (ﷺ) said, "There is nothing that Allāh ordains for the believer except that it is good for him. If he encounters times of ease, he is grateful and that is good for him. If he encounters misfortune, he is patient and that is good for him. This only holds true for the believer."[10]

It is from this vantage point that the Gnostics do not choose one state to the exclusion of the other, instead they are content with whichever has been decreed by Allāh, and they establish that servitude which is befitting each situation.

The *Musnad* and Tirmidhī record the ḥadīth of Abū Umāmah that the Prophet (ﷺ) said, "My Lord offered to make the plain and pebbles of Mecca gold but I said, 'No, my Lord! Rather I (would prefer) to eat my fill one day and to go hungry another. When I go hungry, I would turn to You in humble entreaty and remember You, and when I am full, I would thank You and praise You.'"[11]

'Umar said, 'I care not if I awake in a state that I like or dislike since I do not know in which of the two states goodness lies.'[12]

---

[10] Muslim #2999 on the authority of Ṣuhayb ibn Sinān

[11] Aḥmad #22190 and Tirmidhī #2347 who said it was ḥasan.
Albānī, *Taḥqiq Bidāyatu'l-Sūl*, pg. 63 ruled the first part of the ḥadīth to be authentic due to supporting witnesses and the second part commencing with "I would be full..." to be munkar; Arna'ūṭ said that the isnād was ḍa'īf jiddan.

[12] Ibn Abi al-Dunyā, *al-Faraj ba'd al-Shiddah*, pg. 21

'Umar ibn Abdu'l-'Azīz said, 'I awoke one morning to find that my delight and relief lay in the workings of the ordainment and decree.'

O person! Why is it that when We summon you, you flee from Us?! We shower blessings on you yet you forget Us and remain heedless! We afflict you with tribulation that you may return to Us, that you may stand at Our threshold and humbly entreat Us! Tribulation brings you and Us together, well-being brings you together with your self!

Even if we rebuke each other,
Or we each move to distant lands,
The love you know will still exist
The blessings you know remain abundant
Many are the gifts shrouded in calamity:
'Many are the secrets hidden in recesses.'

O person, your gratitude for Our blessings is in itself a blessing conferred by Us, so be grateful for it! If you are patient in the face of tribulation, patience is a grace We have conferred upon you, so make mention of it! Every circumstance you pass through is a blessing from Us, so be not ungrateful!

وَإِن تَعُدُّوا۟ نِعْمَتَ ٱللَّهِ
لَا تُحْصُوهَآ ۗ إِنَّ ٱلْإِنسَـٰنَ لَظَلُومٌ كَفَّارٌ ﴿٣٤﴾

"If you tried to number Allāh's blessings, you could never count them. Man is indeed wrong-doing, ungrateful."[13]

[13] *Ibrāhīm* (14): 34

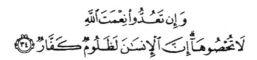

If my gratitude is a blessing awarded
One must then display appreciation.
How can gratitude not be His gift granted?
Days fly by, years accumulate:
If a person sees ease, joyous are they,
If he sees hardship, reward soon ensues.
In both cases, He confers such grace
As cannot be girded by belief, land or sea.

Here ends the treatise by the grace of Allāh, His providence and His divine accord.
All praise is due to Allāh.

APPENDIX ONE

Ḥadīth Sourcing

There are numerous routes to the ḥadīth of ibn 'Abbās

1. The route of Ḥanash al-Ṣana'ānī from ibn 'Abbās with the words, 'One day, I was sitting behind the Messenger of Allāh when he said, "Young lad, I will relate some words to you: Safeguard Allāh and He will safeguard you. Safeguard Allāh and you will find Him before you. When you ask, ask Allāh. When you seek aid, turn to Allāh. If the nation were to come in order to benefit you with something that Allāh has not decreed for you, they would not be able to; and if they desired to harm you with something that Allāh has not decreed for you, they would not be able to. The Pens have been lifted and the books have dried."

This was recorded by Aḥmad #2669-2763, ibn Wahb, *al-Qadr* #28, Tirmidhī #2516 and the wording is his. He said it was ḥasan ṣaḥīḥ.

A similar wording is recorded by Ṭabarānī, *al-Du'ā* #42 via the route of 'Abdullāh al-Ṣāliḥ.

It is recorded by Aḥmad #2803, Bayhaqī, *Shu'ab al-Īmān* #1074 via the route of Ḥanash with the words, 'I was sitting behind the Prophet (ﷺ) when he said, "Young lad, should I not teach you some words through which Allāh will occasion benefit for you?" I said, "Of course!" He said, "Safeguard Allāh and He will safeguard you. Safeguard Allāh and you will find Him in front of you. Know Allāh in times of ease and He will know you in times of hardship. When you ask, ask Allāh. When you seek aid, turn to Allāh. The Pen has dried (after having written) all that will occur. If the whole of creation, in its entirety, was to try and effectuate some benefit for you through something that Allāh has not decreed, they would not be able to do so; and if they wished to harm you through something that Allāh has not decreed, they would not be able to do so. Know that great good lies in bearing with patience what you dislike, that victory comes with patience, that relief comes with distress, and that with hardship comes ease."'

2. The route of Ismā'īl ibn 'Ayyāsh, from 'Umar ibn 'Abdullāh, the freed slave of Ghufrah, from 'Ikrimah, from ibn 'Abbās who said, 'I was sitting behind the Prophet (ﷺ) when he said, "Young lad, should I not teach you some words through which Allāh will occasion benefit for you?" I said, "Of course!" He said, "Safeguard Allāh and He will safeguard you. Safeguard Allāh and you will find Him in front of you. Know Allāh in times of ease and He will know you in times of hardship. When you ask, ask Allāh. When you seek aid, turn to Allāh. The Pen has dried (after having written) all that will occur. If the whole of creation, in its entirety, was to strive in effectuating some benefit for you through something that Allāh has not decreed, they would not be able to do so; and if they strove to harm you through something that Allāh has not decreed, they would not be able to do so. Know that great good lies in bearing with patience what you dislike,

that victory comes with patience, that relief comes with distress, and that with hardship comes ease.'"

This was recorded by Ṭabarānī, *al-Kabīr*, vol. 11. pg. 223

3. The route of ibn Abī Mulaykah from ibn 'Abbās who said that the Messenger of Allāh (ﷺ) said, "Young lad, safeguard Allāh and He will safeguard you. Safeguard Allāh and you will find Him in front of you. Know Allāh in times of ease and He will know you in times of hardship. Know that what afflicted you would never have missed you and what missed you would never have afflicted you. If the whole of creation, in its entirety, was to try and give you something that Allāh did not want to come your way, they would not be able to do so; and if it tried to divert something from you that Allāh wanted to afflict you, they would not be able to do so. When you ask, ask Allāh. When you seek aid, turn to Allāh. Know that victory comes with patience, that relief comes with distress, and that with hardship comes ease. Know that the Pen has recorded all that will occur."

This was recorded by 'Uqaylī, vol. 3, pp. 397-398, Ṭabarānī, *al-Kabīr*, vol. 11, pg. 123, *al-Du'ā* #41, Bayhaqī, *al-Ādāb* #1073

4. The route of 'Atā' ibn Abū Rabāḥ from ibn 'Abbās that the Messenger of Allāh (ﷺ) said, "Ibn 'Abbās, safeguard Allāh and He will safeguard you. Safeguard Allāh and you will find Him in front of you. Know Allāh in times of ease and He will know you in times of hardship. Know that what afflicted you would never have missed you and what missed you would never have afflicted you. If the whole of creation, in its entirety, was to try and give you something that Allāh did not want to come your way, they would not be able to do so; and if it tried to divert something

from you that Allāh wanted to afflict you, they would not be able to do so. The Pen has dried (having recorded) all that is to happen until the Day of Rising. When you ask, ask Allāh. When you seek aid, turn to Allāh. Be assured that victory comes with patience, that relief comes with distress, and that with hardship comes ease."

This was recorded by 'Abd ibn Ḥumayd #634 (*al-Muntakhab*).

There is another route to this ḥadīth to 'Aṭā' ibn Abū Rabāḥ to ibn 'Abbās who said, 'While I was sitting behind the Messenger of Allāh (ﷺ), he said, "Young lad, memorise these words from me: Safeguard Allāh and He will safeguard you. Safeguard Allāh and you will find Him before you. When you ask, ask Allāh. When you seek aid, turn to Allāh. The Pens have been lifted and the books have dried. By the One in whose hand is my soul, if the whole of creation, in its entirety, was to strive in trying to harm you with something that Allāh has not decreed for you, they would not be able to."'

This recorded by ibn Abī al-Dunyā, *al-Faraj ba'd al-Shiddah*, 'Uqaylī, vol. 3, pg. 53, Ṭabarānī, *al-Kabīr*, vol. 11, pg. 178

5. The route of 'Ubaydullāh ibn 'Abdullāh from ibn 'Abbās that the Messenger of Allāh (ﷺ) said to him, "Young lad, should I not teach you some words through which Allāh will occasion benefit for you?" I said, "Of course!" He said, "Safeguard Allāh and He will safeguard you. Safeguard Allāh and you will find Him in front of you. Know Allāh in times of ease and He will know you in times of hardship. When you ask, ask Allāh. When you seek aid, turn to Allāh. The Pen has dried (after having written) all that will occur. If the whole of creation, in its entirety, was to

try and give you something that Allāh, Mighty and Magnificent, has not decreed, they would not be able to do so; and if they they tried to prevent something that Allāh, Mighty and Magnificent, has decreed for you, they would not be able to do so. If you are able to work deeds for the sake of Allāh, being content and in a state of certainty, do so. Know that great good lies in bearing with patience what you dislike, that victory comes with patience, that relief comes with distress, and that with hardship comes ease.'"

This was recorded by Abū Nu'aym, vol. 1, pg. 314

6. The route of 'Abdu'l-Malik ibn 'Umayr from ibn 'Abbās that the Prophet (ﷺ) said, to him, "Young lad!" He replied, 'I am here, Messenger of Allāh, attentive.' He said, "Safeguard Allāh and He will safeguard you. Safeguard Allāh and you will find Him in front of you. Know Allāh in times of ease and He will know you in times of hardship. When you ask, ask Allāh. When you seek aid, turn to Allāh. The Pen has dried (after having written) all that will occur. If people were to strive in benefiting you with something that Allāh has not ordained, they would not be able to do so; and if they tried to harm you with something that Allāh has not decreed for you, they would not be able to do so. If you are able to work deeds for the sake of Allāh, being content and in a state of certainty, do so. If you are unable, know that great good lies in bearing with patience what you dislike, that victory comes with patience, that relief comes with distress, and that with hardship comes ease.'"

This was recorded by Ḥakim #6303

7. The route of Ḥajjāj ibn al-Furāḍah from ibn 'Abbās

8. The route of Humām ibn Yaḥyā al-Baṣrī from ibn 'Abbās

These two have the same wording as #1 above and are recorded by Aḥmad #2803.

The ḥadīth of 'Alī is recorded by Tinnawkhī, *al-Faraj ba'd al-Shiddah*, vol. 1, pg. 112 with a ḍā'īf jiddan isnād since it contains 'Alī ibn Abū 'Alī who is matrūk. cf. al-Mīzān, vol. 3, pg. 147.

The ḥadīth of Sahl ibn Sa'd is recorded by ibn Abī al-Dunyā, *al-Faraj ba'd al-Shiddah* and Tinnawkhī, *al-Faraj ba'd al-Shiddah* , vol. 1, pg. 112 with a ḍa'īf isnād. Suyūṭī, *al-Durr al-Manthūr*, vol. 1, pg. 159 references it to Dāruquṭnī, *Afrād*, ibn Mardawayh, Bayhaqī and Aṣbahānī.

The ḥadīth of Abū Sa'īd al-Khudrī is recorded by Abū Ya'lā #1099, ibn Ad2, vol. 7, pg. 2683 with a ḍa'īf jiddan isnād since it contains Yaḥyā ibn Maymūn ibn 'Aṭā' who is matrūk, and 'Alī ibn Zayd ibn Jud'ān who is ḍa'īf.

The ḥadīth is also recorded from 'Abdullāh ibn Ja'far by ibn Abī 'Āṣim #315 with a ḍa'īf isnād.

APPENDIX TWO

Ibn al-Qayyim on Patience

Allāh, Glorious and Most High, has made patience a race horse that never falters or stumbles, a sword that never loses its sharpness, a vanquishing army that is never defeated, and a fortified stronghold that never breaks and is never taken by force. Patience and divine help are two blood brothers.

Divine help comes with patience, relief follows difficulty, and ease follows hardship. Patience aids and supports a person more than an army of people, and in the attainment of victory it is like the head to the body. In His Book, the Truthful Guarantor has promised that He will repay the patient with a reward that knows no bounds; He informed us that He is with the patient through His guiding them, aiding them and granting them clear victory. He, Most High, says,

وَٱصۡبِرُوٓاْۚ إِنَّ ٱللَّهَ مَعَ ٱلصَّٰبِرِينَ ﴿٤٦﴾

"And be steadfast, Allāh is with the steadfast."[1]

The patient are victorious by virtue of this 'withness' both in

---

[1] *al-Anfāl* (8): 46

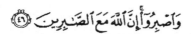

this life and the next, and through it they attain His internal and external blessings.

Allāh made leadership in the religion dependant upon patience and certainty,

وَجَعَلْنَا مِنْهُمْ أَئِمَّةً يَهْدُونَ
بِأَمْرِنَا لَمَّا صَبَرُوا۟ وَكَانُوا۟ بِـَٔايَـٰتِنَا يُوقِنُونَ ﴿٢٤﴾

"We appointed leaders from among them, guiding by Our command when they were patient and when they had certainty about Our signs."[2]

He informed us that patience is best for the patient, consolidating this reality by taking an oath,

وَلَئِن صَبَرْتُمْ لَهُوَ خَيْرٌ لِّلصَّـٰبِرِينَ ﴿١٢٦﴾

"But if you are patient, it is better to be patient."[3]

He informed us that the plots of the enemy are of no avail against the one who has patience and *taqwā*,

وَإِن تَصْبِرُوا۟ وَتَتَّقُوا۟ لَا يَضُرُّكُمْ كَيْدُهُمْ شَيْـًٔا

"But if you are steadfast and have *taqwā*, their scheming will not harm you in any way."[4]

---

[2] *al-Sajdah* (32): 24

[3] *al-Naḥl* (16): 126

[4] *Āli 'Imrān* (3): 120

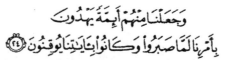

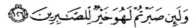

He informed us that it was the patience and *taqwā* of his truthful Prophet, Yūsuf, that led him to circumstances of nobility and authority,

مَن يَتَّقِ وَيَصْبِرْ فَإِنَّ ٱللَّهَ لَا يُضِيعُ أَجْرَ ٱلْمُحْسِنِينَ ﴿٩٠﴾

"As for those who fear Allāh and are patient, Allāh does not allow to go to waste the wage of a people who do good."[5]

Success is dependent on patience and *taqwā*,

يَٰٓأَيُّهَا ٱلَّذِينَ ءَامَنُوا۟ ٱصْبِرُوا۟ وَصَابِرُوا۟ وَرَابِطُوا۟ وَٱتَّقُوا۟ ٱللَّهَ لَعَلَّكُمْ تُفْلِحُونَ ﴿٢٠٠﴾

"You who have faith! Be patient; be supreme in patience; be firm on the battlefield; and have *taqwā* of Allāh so that hopefully you will be successful."[6]

He, Most High, gave the greatest encouragement possible concerning patience to those who desire Him saying,

وَٱللَّهُ يُحِبُّ ٱلصَّٰبِرِينَ ﴿١٤٦﴾

"Allāh loves the patient."[7]

---

[5] *Yūsuf* (12): 90

[6] *Āli 'Imrān* (3): 200

[7] *Āli 'Imran* (3): 146

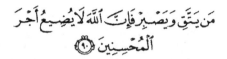

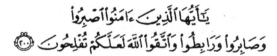

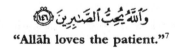

He gave glad-tidings to the patient of three things; each of these things being better than anything that could be envied in this world,

وَبَشِّرِ ٱلصَّٰبِرِينَ ﴿١٥٥﴾ ٱلَّذِينَ إِذَآ أَصَٰبَتْهُم مُّصِيبَةٌ قَالُوٓا۟ إِنَّا لِلَّهِ وَإِنَّآ إِلَيْهِ رَٰجِعُونَ
﴿١٥٦﴾ أُو۟لَٰٓئِكَ عَلَيْهِمْ صَلَوَٰتٌ مِّن رَّبِّهِمْ وَرَحْمَةٌ ۖ وَأُو۟لَٰٓئِكَ
هُمُ ٱلْمُهْتَدُونَ ﴿١٥٧﴾

"But give good news to the patient: those who, when disaster strikes them, say, 'We belong to Allāh and to Him we will return.' Those are the people who will have blessings and mercy from their Lord; they are the ones who are guided."[8]

He enjoined His servants to seeking aid through patience and prayer when facing the vicissitudes of the world and religion,

وَٱسْتَعِينُوا۟ بِٱلصَّبْرِ وَٱلصَّلَوٰةِ ۚ وَإِنَّهَا لَكَبِيرَةٌ إِلَّا عَلَى ٱلْخَٰشِعِينَ

"Seek help in patience and prayer. But that is a very hard thing, except for the humble."[9]

He declared that the grant of victory by way of Paradise and deliverance from the Fire is only for the patient,

إِنِّى جَزَيْتُهُمُ ٱلْيَوْمَ بِمَا صَبَرُوٓا۟ أَنَّهُمْ هُمُ ٱلْفَآئِزُونَ ﴿١١١﴾

---

[8] *al-Baqarah* (2): 155-157

[9] *al-Baqarah* (2): 45

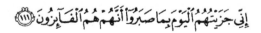

> **"Today I have rewarded them for being steadfast. They are the ones who are victorious."[10]**

He informed us that the desire for His reward and turning away from this world and its allures can only be attained by the patient believer,

ٱلَّذِينَ أُوتُوا۟ ٱلْعِلْمَ وَيْلَكُمْ ثَوَابُ ٱللَّهِ خَيْرٌ لِّمَنْ ءَامَنَ
وَعَمِلَ صَٰلِحًا وَلَا يُلَقَّىٰهَآ إِلَّا ٱلصَّٰبِرُونَ ﴿٨٠﴾

> **"But those who had been given knowledge said, 'Woe to you! Allāh's reward is better for those who have faith and act rightly. But only the steadfast will obtain it.'"[11]**

Returning an evil with that which is better transforms an enemy into a close friend,

وَلَا تَسْتَوِى ٱلْحَسَنَةُ وَلَا ٱلسَّيِّئَةُ ۚ
ٱدْفَعْ بِٱلَّتِى هِىَ أَحْسَنُ فَإِذَا ٱلَّذِى بَيْنَكَ وَبَيْنَهُۥ عَدَٰوَةٌ كَأَنَّهُۥ
وَلِىٌّ حَمِيمٌ ﴿٣٤﴾

> **"...Repel the bad with something better and, if there is enmity between you and someone else, he will be like a bosom friend."[12]**

---

[10] *al-Mu'minūn* (23): 111

[11] *al-Qaṣaṣ* (28): 80

[12] *Fuṣṣilat* (41): 34

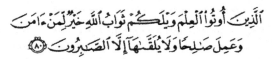

None will attain this quality but those who are truly patient. None will obtain it but those who have great good fortune.[13]

Allāh, Most High, informed us - making an oath to further stress what is being said,

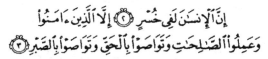

إِنَّ ٱلْإِنسَٰنَ لَفِى خُسْرٍ ﴿٢﴾ إِلَّا ٱلَّذِينَ ءَامَنُوا۟
وَعَمِلُوا۟ ٱلصَّٰلِحَٰتِ وَتَوَاصَوْا۟ بِٱلْحَقِّ وَتَوَاصَوْا۟ بِٱلصَّبْرِ ﴿٣﴾

"Truly man is in loss - except for those who have faith and do right actions and urge each other to the truth and urge each other to patience."[14]

He divided the creation in two groups: the People of the Right and the People of the Left. He particularised the People of the Right to be those who urge each other to patience and mercy[15] and particularised the patient and grateful as those who truly benefit from his Signs. He said in four verses of His Book,

إِنَّ فِى ذَٰلِكَ لَءَايَٰتٍ لِّكُلِّ صَبَّارٍ شَكُورٍ ﴿٣١﴾

"There are certainly Signs in that for everyone who is patient and thankful."[16]

He made forgiveness and reward dependent on righteous deeds

---

[13] Redacted from *Fuṣṣilat* (41): 35

[14] *al-'Aṣr* (103): 2-3

[15] *al-Balad* (90): 17

[16] *Luqmān* (31): 31; *Ibrāhīm* (14): 5; *Saba'* (34): 19; *al-Shūrā* (42): 33

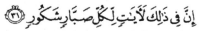

and patience - and that is truly easy for the one for whom He facilitates the way,

إِلَّا ٱلَّذِينَ صَبَرُوا۟ وَعَمِلُوا۟ ٱلصَّٰلِحَٰتِ أُو۟لَٰٓئِكَ لَهُم مَّغْفِرَةٌ
وَأَجْرٌ كَبِيرٌ ﴿١١﴾

> **"Except for those who are patient and do right actions. They will receive forgiveness and a large reward."**[17]

Patience and forgiveness are one of the resolute and definite matters such that the one who trades in them will never face loss,

وَلَمَن صَبَرَ وَغَفَرَ إِنَّ ذَٰلِكَ لَمِنْ عَزْمِ ٱلْأُمُورِ

> **"But if someone is patient and forgives, that is the most resolute course to follow."**[18]

He ordered His Messenger to be patient for His judgment and informed us that patience can only be for His sake, and through this all calamities become relatively minor and easy to bear,

وَٱصْبِرْ لِحُكْمِ رَبِّكَ فَإِنَّكَ بِأَعْيُنِنَا

> **"So be patient for the judgment of your Lord - you are certainly before Our eyes"**[19]

---

[17] *Hūd* (11): 11

[18] *al-Shūrā* (42): 43

[19] *al-Ṭūr* (52): 48

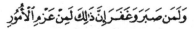

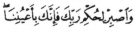

وَٱصْبِرْ وَمَا صَبْرُكَ إِلَّا بِٱللَّهِ
وَلَا تَحْزَنْ عَلَيْهِمْ وَلَا تَكُ فِى ضَيْقٍ مِّمَّا يَمْكُرُونَ
﴿١٢٧﴾ إِنَّ ٱللَّهَ مَعَ ٱلَّذِينَ ٱتَّقَوا۟ وَّٱلَّذِينَ هُم مُّحْسِنُونَ ﴿١٢٨﴾

"Be patient. But your patience is only with Allāh. Do not be grieved by them and do not be constricted by the plots they hatch. Allāh is with those who have *taqwā* of Him and with those who do good."[20]

Patience is the noose of the believer, tying him down: he may wander for a bit but always returns. It is the pillar of his faith to which he recourses: there is no faith for the one who has no patience. If, in such a case, it does exist, it would be severely weak. The one who has no patience is like one worshipping Allāh at the edge of a faltering precipice: if good comes his way he takes comfort, but if trial comes his way, the world turns inside out and he loses both it and the Hereafter.

The best livelihood that the felicitous attained was because of their patience. They rose to the most exalted stations because of their gratitude.[21] On the wings of patience and gratitude they

---

[20] *al-Nahl* (16): 127-128

[21] *Shukr*: praising another for the good that he has done to one. Ibn al-Qayyim, *Madārij*, vol. 2, pg. 244 said, '*Shukr* is to display the effects of the blessings of Allāh upon the tongue by way of praise and acknowledgment; in the heart by way of witnessing and love; and upon the limbs by way of submission and obedience.' Fairozabādī, Baṣā'ir, said that *shukr* was built upon five pillars: submission to the One who gave the blessings; loving Him; acknowledging His blessing; praising

=

soared to the Gardens of perpetual bliss. That is the grace of Allāh which He bestows on whoever He will, He is the possessor of great grace.

Faith is of two halves: patience and gratitude. As such it is befitting for one who is sincere to himself, who desires his soul to succeed, and gives preference to its being felicitous that he not ignore these two principles, and not swerve from these two paths. In this way Allāh would place him in the better of the two parties on the Day of His meeting.

Later on, defining patience, ibn al-Qayyim writes:

It is a noble mannerism of the soul that prevents it from doing that which is not good or pleasing; it is a quality of the soul which leads to its correction and rectification.

Junayd ibn Muḥammad was asked about it to which he replied, 'It means swallowing gall without a frown.' Dhū'l-Nūn said, 'Patience is to keep your distance from opposing (the commands of Allāh), to remain silent and composed while swallowing hefty portions of tribulation, and to show independence although poverty strikes you in every field of life.' It is also said, 'Patience is

---

=

Him for it; and not using it in any way that may displease Him.

Ibn Ḥajr, *Fatḥ al-Bārī*, vol. 11, pg. 311 said, '*Shukr* comprises *ṣabr* upon obedience and away from disobedience. Some of the Imāms said that *ṣabr* necessitates *shukr* and cannot be completed without it, and the opposite; hence if one of them goes so too does the other. So whoever is in a state of receiving favours, it is obligatory upon him to show *ṣabr* and *shukr*, *ṣabr* from disobedience. Whoever is in a state of trial, it is also obligatory upon him to show *ṣabr* and *shuker*, *shukr* by establishing the rights of Allāh during that trial. Indeed servitude is due to Allāh in times of tribulation and in times of ease.'

to meet tribulation with fine conduct.' It is also said, 'Patience is to vanish in tribulation without manifesting complaint.' Abū 'Uthmān said, 'The continuously patient is one who has accustomed his soul to meet the onslaught of difficult circumstances.'

It is also said, 'Patience is to face tribulation with fine fellowship just as one would face times of ease and well-being.' The meaning of this is that servitude is due to Allāh in times of ease and hardship, as such he must accompany well-being with gratitude and tribulation with patience.

'Amr ibn 'Uthmān al-Makkī said, 'Patience is to stand firm with Allāh and to meet His tribulations with composure and welcome.' The meaning of this is that one meets tribulation with an equanimity that contains no constriction, anger or complaint.

Khawāṣ said, 'Patience is to remain firm to the regulations of the Book and Sunnah.' Ruwaym said, 'Patience is to abandon complaint.' Hence he explained it by its outcome.

Other said, 'Patience is to seek help from Allāh.' Abū 'Alī said, 'Patience is like its name.'[22]

'Alī ibn Ṭālib, may Allāh be well pleased with him, said, 'Patience is a stead that does not stumble or falter.'

Abū Muḥammad al-Jarīrī said, 'Patience is to not differentiate between a state of blessing and a state of trial, with peace of mind in both.' I say: neither is this possible nor is it required for

---

[22] The author, may Allāh have mercy upon him, has already mentioned in the previous chapter that *ṣabr* is also the name of a very bitter medicine.

Allāh has created us in a way that our very nature distinguishes between the two states. What is required, however, is to restrain the soul from despair and complaint. The arena of well-being is easier than the arena of patience as the Prophet (ﷺ) said in his famous supplication, "As long as You are not angry with me, I care not, but I would prefer Your state of well-being."[23]

This does not contradict his (ﷺ) saying, "None has been granted a gift better and greater than patience,"[24] for after the occurrence of tribulation, the servant has nothing at his disposal that is better or greater than patience. However, before the occurrence of tribulation, well-being is better for him.

Abū 'Alī al-Daqqāq said, 'The definition of patience is that you not object to the decree. However, allowing the effects of tribulation to show, without complaining, does not go against patience. Allāh, Most High, says concerning Ayyūb, *"We found him patient,"*[25] despite the fact that he said, *"Great harm has afflicted me."*[26]'

I say: he explained the word by its consequences. With regards his saying, 'without complaining,' complaint is of two types:

The first: complaining to Allāh, this does not go against pa-

---

[23] Ṭabarānī, vol.13, pg. 73 #181. This is the famous supplication that he said after returning from Ṭā'if.

[24] Bukhārī #1469-6470, Muslim #1053 on the authority of Abū Sa'īd.

[25] *Ṣād* (38): 44

[26] *al-Anbiyā'* (21): 83

tience. Ya'qūb said, *"I make complaint about my grief and sorrow to Allāh Alone,"*[27] despite his already having said, *"beauty lies in showing patience,"*[28] and Allāh having described him as a patient person.

The Master of the Patient (ﷺ) said, "Allāh! It is to You that I complain of my weakness and lack of resources..."[29]

Mūsā (*'alayhis-salām*) said, "Allāh, to You belongs all praise and to You does one complain. You are the One who aids, through You does one seek relief, upon You does one rely, and there is no power or strength except through You."

The second: that the one undergoing affliction complains either verbally or in some other more indirect way, this cannot coexist with patience, rather it goes against it. There is a clear distinction between complaining to Him and complaining about the tribulation. We shall analyse this in detail later.

It is said, 'Patience is courage of the soul.' It is from this state-

[27] *Yūsuf* (12): 86

[28] *Yūsuf* (12): 13, 83

[29] A part of the supplication after Ṭā'if; cf. fn. #23.
The full text of the supplication reads, "Allāh, I complain to You about my weakness and lack of resources. O You, most Merciful of all, You who are the Lord of the oppressed, You are my Lord, to whom would You entrust me, to those far away who greet me with displeasure, or to some enemy? As long as You are not angry with me, I care not, but I would prefer Your state of well-being. I take refuge with the light of Your face that brightens shadows, repairs the troubles of this world and the Hereafter, ensuring that Your anger or discontent not alight upon me. May You be content and be pleased; all power and strength stems from You."

ment that the phrase, 'Courage is to show patience for an hour,' derives. It is said, 'Patience is the heart remaining calm at restless times.'

Patience and despair are two opposites and they are mentioned in contrasting contexts. Allāh, Most High, says,

سَوَآءٌ عَلَيْنَآ أَجَزِعْنَآ أَمْ صَبَرْنَا مَا لَنَا مِن مَّحِيصٍ ﴿٢١﴾

"It makes no difference whether we cannot stand it or bear patiently, we have no way of escape."[30]

Despair is the partner of inability and inadequacy whereas patience is the partner of intelligence and sagacity. Were despair to be asked, 'Who is you father?' it would reply, 'Inability'; and were patience to be asked, 'Who is your father?' it would reply, 'Sagacity.'

The soul is the mount of the servant upon which he embarks either to Paradise or Hell. Patience is like the rein of that mount, and were there to be no rein, the mount would bolt here and there, directionless.

In one of his sermons, Ḥajjāj said, 'Restrain these souls for they plunge into every evil. May Allāh have mercy upon a person who places a rein around his soul and guides it to the obedience of Allāh and turns it away from disobedience. Know that patiently staying away from what Allāh has prohibited is easier than bearing His punishment!'

I say: the soul has the ability of driving and daring, and the

[30] *Ibrāhīm* (14): 21

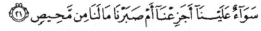

ability of restraint and desistance. The reality of patience is that one directs its driving force towards that which would benefit him and directs its desistance towards that which would harm him.

Some people find that their ability to patiently persevere in doing that which will benefit them is greater than their ability to patiently refrain from that which will harm them. As such they are able to persevere in fulfilling the commandments but are unable to restrain their desires such that they stay away from the prohibitions. Other people find that their ability to patiently refrain from opposition is greater than their ability to patiently persevere in obedience. Yet others are unable to do either of the two.

The best person is the one who has most patience in both matters. Many people are able to persevere in praying by night, be it hot or cold, and fast by day, but are unable to lower their gazes. Many people are able to lower their gaze but are unable to enjoin the good and forbid evil or undertake Jihād. The majority of people are unable to show patience in both matters and a minority are able to show befitting patience in both cases.

It is said, 'Patience is that intellect and religion stand firm when faced with lusts and desires.' The meaning of this is that human nature runs after that which it loves, but intellect and religion prevent it. As such the two are at continuous war with each other, and this war has its ups and downs. The battlefield is the heart, patience, courage and firmness.[31]

---

[31] Ibn al-Qayyim, *'Idatu'l-Ṣābirīn wa Dhakīratu'l-Shākirīn*

APPENDIX THREE

The Benefits of Tribulation
al-'Izz ibn 'Abdu'l-Salām

In tribulations, trials, misfortunes and calamities lie a number of benefits; these benefits have differing degrees of relevance, differing in accordance to the various ranks of people.

- Realising the greatness of Allāh's Lordship and His all-encompassing power.

- Realising the humility and dejection of servitude.

- Actualising sincerity for Allāh, Most High. This is because there is no way to repress hardship except by recoursing to Him and there is no one that one can depend on to remove it except Him.

- Turning in penitence to Allāh, Most High, and directing ones heart to Him.

- Submissiveness and supplication.

- Forbearance.[1] The ranking of forbearance differs in accordance to the magnitude of calamity; showing forbearance at the onset of the severest calamities is from its greatest manifestations.

- Patience and steadfastness in the face of affliction, this leads to Allāh's love and increase in His rewards.

- Experiencing joy at the onset of calamity because of the many benefits it contains.

- Being grateful at the onset of calamity because of the many benefits it contains. Comparable to this is the case of a sick person thanking a doctor who has just amputated one of his limbs in order to save his life, even though this would serve to disable him to some extent.

- Its expiating sins and errors.

- Showing mercy to those who are undergoing affliction and coming to their aid.

- Understanding the greatness of the blessing of ease and well-being. This is because blessings are never truly appreciated until one loses them.

- Understanding what Allāh, Most High, has caused to be

[1] *Ḥilm*: the abandonment of haste. Rāghib, *al-Mufradāt* said, 'It is the ability to control the soul and temperament at the onrush of anger.' Jāhiẓ, *Tahdhib al-Akhlāq* said, 'It is the abandonment of taking revenge in the state of extreme anger, despite the ability to do so.' Jurjānī, *al-Ta'rīfāt* said, 'It is to be calm in the state of anger.'

the outcome of these benefits in terms of reward in the Hereafter.

- Realising the many hidden benefits it contains. When the tyrannical ruler took Sārah from Ibrāhīm, one of the hidden benefits of this trial was that later she was given Hājar as a servant who bore Ibrāhīm, Ismā'īl, from whose progeny was born the Master of the Messengers and the Seal of the Prophets (ﷺ). Look and see how great the hidden benefit was in that trial!

- Tribulation and hardship prevents one from evil, vanity, boastfulness, arrogance, ostentation and oppression. It is because of these great benefits that those who were tried most severely were the Prophets, then the righteous and then those closest to them.[2] They were accused of being mad, magicians, fortune tellers; they were mocked and ridiculed. The Companions were evicted from their homes and lands, forced to flee leaving their possessions behind them, their tribulations went from severity to severity, their enemies multiplied in number, on occasion they were overcome and defeated, many of them were killed at Uḥud and other places and battles, the Messenger of Allāh (ﷺ) received injury in his face, one of his molar teeth was broken and his helmet was crushed into the sides of his head and split to expose his head; his enemies rejoiced and his associates despaired. They would live in a constant state of fear, destitution and poverty. They

[2] Aḥmad #1481-1494-1555-1607, Tirmidhī #2400, ibn Mājah #4023 on the authority of Sa'd ibn Abū Waqqāṣ.

Tirmidhī said it was ḥasan ṣaḥīḥ, Ḥākim #120 said it was ṣaḥīḥ and Dhahabi agreed.

would be forced to tie rocks to their stomachs out of severe hunger[3] and the Master of the first and last never ate his fill of bread twice in any one day.[4] He was injured in various ways to the point that they accused the chastity of his most beloved wife. The Prophets and righteous have always faced trials and tribulations, with each person being tried in proportion to his religion. Some of them would be sawn in half but this would not make them renegade from their faith. The state of hardship and tribulation causes the servant to turn towards Allāh, Mighty and Magnificent.[5] The state of ease, well-being and blessings causes the servant to turn away from Allāh. This is why they ate scarcely and wore modest clothing etc. so that they could be in a state that would lead them to turn back to Allāh, Mighty and Magnificent, and devote themselves to Him.

- Being pleased and content with the tribulation such that it would lead to the pleasure of Allāh, Most High. This is because both the righteous and sinner is afflicted with trial, hence whoever is malcontent at its onset, for him is displeasure and misery in this life and the Hereafter. Whoever is pleased and content with it, for him lies in store the good pleasure of

[3] Bukhārī #6452 on the authority of Abū Hurayrah.

[4] Muslim #2970 on the authority of 'Ā'ishah.

[5] Munāwī, *Fayḍ al-Qadīr*, vol.1, pg. 245 said, 'Ghazālī said, "If you see Allāh, Mighty and Magnificent, holding back this world from you, frequently trying you with adversity and tribulation, know that you hold a great status with Him. Know that He is dealing with you as he does with His *Awlīyā'* and chosen elite and is watching over you, have you not heard His saying, **"So wait steadfastly for the judgment of your Lord - you are certainly before Our eyes"** [*al-Ṭūr* (52): 48], so acknowledge this great favour upon you."'

Allāh and that is greater than Paradise and what it contains.[6]

[6] Summarised from his work, *Fawā'id al-Balwā w'al-Miḥan*, the full translation of which has been published by Daar al-Sunnah Publishers 2004, Birmingham, United Kingdom under the title, Trials & Tribulations: Wisdom & Benefits.

APPENDIX FOUR

'Alī al-Qarī's Commentary

al-Mishkāt #5302 records the ḥadīth in which ibn 'Abbās (*raḍiyAllāhu 'anhumā*) said, 'I was sitting behind the Prophet (ﷺ) when he said, "Young lad: Safeguard Allāh and He will safeguard you. Safeguard Allāh and you will find Him before you. When you ask, ask Allāh. When you seek aid, turn to Allāh. Know that if the nation came together in order to benefit you with something, they would not be able to do so except with something that Allāh has decreed for you; and were they to come together in order to harm you with something, they would not be able to do so except with something that Allāh has decreed against you. The Pens have been lifted and the scrolls have dried."

'Alī al-Qārī, *Mirqāt al-Mafātīḥ Sharḥ Mishkāt al-Maṣābīḥ*, vol. 9, pp. 161-166, wrote,

"I was sitting behind the Prophet (ﷺ)," this indicates that (ibn 'Abbās) memorised the incident accurately, brought the words to mind and accurately conveyed them. This is one of the ḥadīths that he heard from the Messenger of Allāh (ﷺ) directly for most of what he narrates is via the medium of another narrator, however these

are taken as proof because they are the mursal narrations of a Companion (which are accepted). The reason for this is that he was very young during the time of the Prophet (ﷺ). The author (Baghawī) said that he was born three years before the Hijra and he was thirteen years old when the Prophet (ﷺ) passed away, some said that he was fifteen at the time and yet others said he was ten. However, despite this he became a great scholar and the ocean of knowledge of this nation because the Prophet (ﷺ) supplicated that he acquire wisdom,[1] understanding and correct interpretation.[2] He saw Jibrīl twice[3] and he became blind at the end of his life. He passed away at Ṭā'if in the year 68H during the rule of ibn al-Zubayr at the age of seventy one. A large number of Companions and Successors narrate from him.

"Young lad," the point behind the address is to encourage ibn 'Abbās to direct his attention to him and pay heed to what was to follow. In *al-Adhkār*, mentioned next are the words, *"I will teach you some words...,"* i.e. points of advice that will be of benefit in curbing affliction and promoting benefit and blessings.

"Safeguard Allāh," i.e. His command and His prohibition. *"He will safeguard you,"* He will safeguard you in this worldly life by keeping you away from its pitfalls and calamities. He will safeguard you in the Hereafter from the various types of punishment

---

[1] Bukhārī #75-143-3756-7270 on the authority of ibn 'Abbās

[2] Aḥmad #2397-2879-3032-3102 with an isnād meeting the criteria of Muslim as stated by Arna'ūṭ. It was ruled ṣaḥīḥ by ibn Ḥibbān #3711, ibn Khuzaymah #2736 and Ḥākim #6280 with Dhahabī agreeing.
cf. Aḥmad #1840-2422-3022-3060

[3] Tirmidhī #3822 and he said that it was mursal.

and the levels of Hell: a goodly, befitting reward since whoever is for Allāh, Allāh is for him.

"Safeguard Allāh," upkeep His rights: always remember Him, always keep Him in mind and be grateful to Him. *"You will find Him before you,"* i.e. in front of you. If you do this, it will be as if He is actually present before you and in front of you. Through the station of beneficence, *iḥsān*, certainty, *yaqīn*, and complete faith, *īmān*, you will witness Him as if your own eyes see Him, obliterating the sight of anything else besides Him in the process. The first is the station of Careful Vigilance, *Murāqabah* and the second is the station of Witnessing, *Mushāhadah*. It is also said that the meaning is that if you preserve and upkeep obedience to Allāh, you will find Him safeguarding you, aiding you in your exigencies and facilitating your affairs for you. It is also said that the meaning is that you will find His providential care and compassion close at hand at all times, and He will tend to you in all circumstances: He will relieve you of all harm and grace you with all types of gifts and favours. This, then alludes to His saying,

وَنَحْنُ أَقْرَبُ إِلَيْهِ مِنْ حَبْلِ الْوَرِيدِ ﴿١٦﴾

"We are nearer to him than his jugular vein."[4]

One of the Gnostics suggested that every single atom in creation is surrounded by, and subjugated to the Light of lights. He is close to it, not just in knowledge, not just by the fact that He brought it into being, but in a way so subtle as to be incompre-

[4] *Qāf* (50): 15

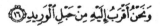

hensible and beyond the ability of words to express,

> When all things vanish in His light
> "Invoke Me, I am close," says He!

Ṭībī, may Allāh have mercy on him, explained the sentence thus, 'Carefully tend to the right of Allāh and seek His good pleasure, then you will find Him before you, i.e. in front of you. Preserve the right of Allāh, Most High, and He will safeguard you from the calamities of this world and the next.'

"When you ask," i.e. when you wish to ask for something, *"ask Allāh,"* alone. The treasures of all providence are with Him, the keys to gifts and all virtue lie in His hand. Every blessing or punishment that reaches the servant or is diverted from him, in this world or the next, is by virtue of His mercy, pure and untainted by personal goal or ulterior motive. This is because He is the absolute and unrestricted Bestower of Good, the Self-Sufficient and Rich who will never be needy or poor. As such, only His mercy must be hoped for, only His punishment must be feared, in times of great adversity, He is to be resorted to, and in the majority of affairs, He is to be relied on. No one else besides Him is to be asked since no one else can grant, withhold, repress harm or promote benefit. *"They have no power to harm or help themselves. They have no power over death or life or resurrection."*[5] In all circumstances, He is to be asked, be it directly or indirectly through ones state and condition.

The ḥadīth states, "Allāh is angry at whoever does not ask of

[5] *al-Furqān* (25): 3

Him."[6] Asking displays ones need of the requested, it acknowledges that one is incapable, needy and indigent. Therefore, a person, instead of affecting the epitome of strength and might, shows abject humility and need. Fine indeed are the words of the poet,

Allāh is angry if you leave asking Him,
The child of Ādam is angry when you ask him.

"When you seek aid," when you want help in obeying Allāh or any affair relating to this world or the Hereafter, *"turn to Allāh,"* for He is the one who aids and, at every time, in every place, trust is to be placed in Him.

"Know," said by way of emphasis so that he be totally attuned to what is being said and hence benefit more, *"that"* if one were to assume, for the sake of argument, *"if the nation came together in order to benefit you with something,"* in your affairs dealing with this life or the next *"they would not be able to do so except with something that Allāh has decreed for you,"* i.e. decreed for you, recorded it in the Remembrance and has finished with it. *"Were they to come together in order to harm you with something,"* i.e. to remove good or promote harm *"they would not be able to do so except with something that Allāh has decreed against you."* The basic meaning is that you must single Allāh out alone for things you want and things you do not want. He is the One who brings about harm and benefit, and grants and with-

[6] Aḥmad #9701, Tirmidhī #3373, ibn Mājah #3827 on the authority of Abū Hurayrah.

Its isnād was ruled ḍa'īf by Dhahabī, *al-Mīzān*, vol. 4, pg. 538 and Arna'ūṭ et. al.

However the ḥadīth was ruled ḥasan due to supports by Albānī, *al-Ṣaḥīḥah* #2654

holds. One of the revealed scriptures mentions, 'By My might and grandeur, I will cut off anyone who places hope in another besides Me. I will clothe him with subjugation amongst his fellow man and I will distance him from My presence and prevent him from reaching Me. I will make him pensive and confused; at times of calamity, hoping in another besides Me whereas all calamities are in My hand. I am the Ever-Living, the Self-Sustaining. He will knock on the doors of others whereas the keys to all doors are in My hands; their doors are locked whereas mine is open to whoever invokes Me.'

"The Pens have been lifted," and are no longer writing the decrees *"and the scrolls have dried,"* having recorded the judgements of creation until the Day of Rising. No Pen will be placed on them again to commence writing anew or to alter something already recorded. Therefore the decrees have all been recorded in the Preserved Tablet and nothing new will now be recorded. The setting of the decree and ordainment has been referred to as the lifting of the Pens and the drying of the scrolls by way of analogy to an author of a book, in this life, completing his work.

We have already discussed the ḥadīth, "The first thing that Allāh created was the Pen which He commanded, 'Write!' In that hour it recorded all that was to happen until the Day of Rising."[7] We have also explained the ḥadīth mentioning that the Pen has dried in accordance to the knowledge of Allāh, meaning that what Allāh knows and has decreed from pre-eternity will not change. One

---

[7] Aḥmad #22705-22707, Abū Dāwūd #4700, Tirmidhī #2155-3319. Tirmidhī said it was ḥasan ṣaḥīḥ gharīb and it was ruled ṣaḥīḥ by ibn al-'Arabī, *Aḥkām al-Qur'ān*, vol. 2, pg. 335, Albānī, *al-Ṣaḥīḥah* #133 and Arna'ūṭ.

should not suppose that this contradicts the saying of Allāh,

يَمْحُوا۟ ٱللَّهُ مَا يَشَآءُ وَيُثْبِتُ ۖ وَعِندَهُۥٓ أُمُّ ٱلْكِتَٰبِ ﴿٣٩﴾

"Allāh erases what He wills or endorses it. The Master Copy of the Book is in His hands."[8]

The erasing or endorsement itself is something recorded and concerning which the scrolls have dried. The ordainment, with respect to the Preserved Tablet, is of two types: irrevocable and conditional. With respect to the knowledge of Allāh it does not change or alter, this is why He says,

وَعِندَهُۥٓ أُمُّ ٱلْكِتَٰبِ ﴿٣٩﴾

"The Master Copy of the Book is in His hands."[9]

It is also said that there are two books with Allāh: the Preserved Tablet which does not change, and a book in which the angel writes and that can change, undergoing erasure or endorsement.

This portion of the ḥadīth was recorded by Tirmidhī and Aḥmad and the former said it was ḥasan ṣaḥīḥ as stated by Nawawī. He then said:

> Another narration, not in Tirmidhī, has, "Safeguard Allāh and you will find Him in front of you. Know Allāh in times of ease and He will know you in times of hardship. Know that what missed you could never

[8] *al-Ra'd* (13): 39

[9] *al-Ra'd* (13): 39

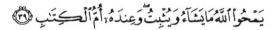

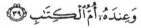

> have afflicted you and what afflicted you could never have missed you." It concludes with the words, "Know that victory comes with patience, that relief comes with distress, and that with hardship comes ease."

"Know Allāh," knowledge leads to love, so the meaning is: endear yourself to Allāh through safeguarding His rules and regulations. This explanation was mentioned by Nawawī, may Allāh have mercy upon him. *"He will know you in times of hardship,"* He will allow you to pass through it unscathed.

"Know that what missed you" of blessing and ease, or tribulation and hardship, *"could never have afflicted you"* ever, it is impossible. *"And what afflicted you could never have missed you,"* as such these statements encourage reliance on Allāh, a state of contentment, and the negation of might and power from oneself. This is because there is no event that occurs be it related to happiness or misery, ease or hardship, good or evil, benefit or harm, lifespan or provision, except that it is dependent on His decree and ordainment which was determined fifty thousand years before He created the heavens and the earth. Movement and stillness are the same. Gratitude must be shown in times of ease and patience in times of adversity since Allāh, Most High, says, "*Say: it is all from Allāh.*"[10]

"Know that victory" against the enemy *"comes with patience,"* in the face of trial and tribulation, *"that relief,"* from sorrow *"comes with distress,"* that strikes at the very heart of man *"and that with hardship comes ease,"* this is also a verse of the Qur'ān which is re-

[10] *al-Nisā'* (4): 78

peated twice. Therefore one learns that every hardship is accompanied with two eases since a well known precept has that if the same indefinite noun is repeated, the repetition is not the same as the original, if a definite noun is repeated, the repetition is the same as the original. However, this principle holds in most cases, not all. Allāh, Most High, says,

قُلِ ٱللَّهُمَّ مَٰلِكَ
ٱلْمُلْكِ تُؤْتِي ٱلْمُلْكَ مَن تَشَآءُ وَتَنزِعُ ٱلْمُلْكَ مِمَّن تَشَآءُ

"Say, 'O Allāh! Master of the Kingdom! You give sovereignty to whoever You will. You take sovereignty from whoever You will...'"[11]

There is no doubt that in the first mention of *al-Mulk* (the Kingdom), the definite article subsumes every single case, whereas in the second mention of *al-mulk* (sovereignty), the definite article expresses the genus of sovereignty and can hold true for isolated instances.

It is said that the meaning of *ma'a*, with, (in the ḥadīth), is *ba'd*, after; but this is far removed from its basic meaning. It is also said that the usage of this word emphasises the essential point: i.e. that one follows the other so closely that it is as if they are together, going hand-in-hand. As such a person can take comfort and solace with this.

However, trials contain many a gift, indeed trials are gifts. Allāh, Most High, says,

[11] *Āli 'Imrān* (3): 26

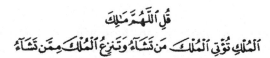

وَفِي ذَٰلِكُم بَلَآءٌ مِّن رَّبِّكُمْ عَظِيمٌ ﴿٤٩﴾

"In that there was a terrible trial from your Lord."[12]

وَمَا يُلَقَّىٰهَآ إِلَّا ٱلَّذِينَ صَبَرُوا۟ وَمَا يُلَقَّىٰهَآ إِلَّا ذُو حَظٍّ عَظِيمٍ ﴿٣٥﴾

"None will obtain it but those who are truly patient. None will obtain it but those who have great good fortune."[13]

The sagacious scholar, the master, 'Abdu'l-Qādir al-Jīlānī, may Allāh sanctify him, said in his *Futūḥāt al-Ghayb*, 'Every believer should make this ḥadīth a mirror to his heart, his axiom, his shelter and his topic of conversation. He should act by it in all times of motion and stillness so that he can be saved in this world and in the Hereafter, finding honour therein by the mercy of Allāh, Most High.'

---

[12] *al-Baqarah* (2): 49

[13] *Fuṣṣilat* (41): 35

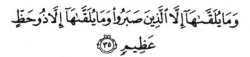

APPENDIX FIVE

Ibn 'Allān's Commentary

Imām Nawawī, *al-Adhkār*, wrote,

> On the authority of ibn 'Abbās (*raḍiyAllāhu 'anhumā*) who said, 'I was sitting behind the Prophet (ﷺ) when he said, "Young lad, I will teach you some words: Safeguard Allāh and He will safeguard you. Safeguard Allāh and you will find Him before you. When you ask, ask Allāh. When you seek aid, turn to Allāh. Know that if the nation came together in order to benefit you with something, they would not be able to do so except with something that Allāh has decreed for you; and were they to come together in order to harm you with something, they would not be able to do so except with something that Allāh has decreed against you. The Pens have been lifted and the scrolls have dried."[1]

This was narrated to us in Tirmidhī and he said it was ḥasan ṣaḥīḥ. Another narration, not in Tirmidhī, has, "Safeguard Allāh and you will find Him in front of

[1] Tirmidhī #2516 who said it was ḥasan ṣaḥīḥ

> you. Know Allāh in times of ease and He will know you in times of hardship. Know that what missed you could never have afflicted you and what afflicted you could never have missed you." It concludes with the words, "Know that victory comes with patience, that relief comes with distress, and that with hardship comes ease."

Ibn 'Allān, *al-Futūḥāt al-Rabbāniyyah 'ala'l-Adhkār al-Nawawiyyah*, vol. 7, pp. 381-389, penned:

"I was sitting behind the Prophet (ﷺ)*,"* on his riding beast as mentioned (explicitly) in another narration. This proves that it is permissible to have more than one person sitting on a beast provided that it is able to bear the weight. The Prophet (ﷺ) had numerous people, forty in total - may Allāh be pleased with them, sit with him on his beast on various occasions and I have written a treatise listing them.[2]

"Young lad," ar: *ghulām*, another narration has the diminutive form, *ghulaym* and is said by way of tenderness and affection, or, here, it could be said by way of respect and hence would be looking forward to what ibn 'Abbās was to become. A child is referred to as a *ghulām* if he has started suckling and is below the age of nine. At the time of this advice, ibn 'Abbās would have been around ten years old, when he (ﷺ) passed away, he was ten or thirteen years old.

"I will teach you some words," which are beneficial; this is explicitly mentioned in another narration, *"through which Allāh will occa-*

---

[2] called *Tuḥfatu'l-Ashrāf bi Ma'rifati'l-Irdāf.*

sion benefit for you." The point of saying this is to prepare the addressee for what is to follow so that the words can have greater impact. This is because, after having said this, the listener will be fully attuned to what follows and eagerly await it. *"Some words,"* ar: *kalimāt* which is a plural imparting the sense of a small number thereby alluding to the fact that the ensuing pieces of advice are short, therefore easy to memorise.[3] This advice collates innumerable regulations, wisdoms and aspect of gnosis; and in his imparting something so important to ibn 'Abbās shows that he (ﷺ) knew what the former was to attain of knowledge and gnosis, the excellence of his conduct and profundity of both his inner and outer states.

"Safeguard Allāh," by safeguarding His religion and command, i.e. obey your Lord, complying with His command, avoiding His prohibition and being cautious of His warnings; if you do this, *"He will safeguard you,"* your self, your family and your worldly life, especially at the point of death. This is because the recompense is of the same type as the deed. This phrase, concise and terse as it may be, subsumes all the regulations contained in the Legal Law, the small and large. It is emphatic and lends a sense of gravity to what is said. As such it is a stark example of the pithiness in speech that Allāh exclusively gave him (ﷺ).[4]

"Safeguard Allāh and you will find Him before you," i.e. in front of

---

[3] The author, *Dalīl al-Fāliḥīn*, vol. 1, pg. 166 adds, 'They are also mentioned in the indefinite form to highlight that fact that they are something momentous and truly important.'

[4] Bukhārī #2977-6998-7013-7273 and Muslim #523 on the authority of Abū Hurayrah

you as mentioned in the second narration. What this means is that you will find Him with you in terms of His preservation, encompassing you, and aiding and supporting you wherever you may be. As such, you will take comfort with Him and you will suffice with Him rather than creation. This phrase emphasises the previous sentence and is a form of rhetoric since a physical direction is impossible for Allāh, Most High. As such it is like the saying of Allāh, *"Allāh is with those who have* taqwā," where the 'withness' is metaphorical, not physical containment. Of the six directions, the direction ahead has been mentioned by way of alluding to a person's goal and intent, and to show that he is travelling to the Hereafter, not permanently residing in this world. A traveller looks in front of him and to what lies ahead. As such the meaning is that (He is with you) wherever you turn, in whatever you intend and want of affairs relating to both abodes. It is also said that this statement is a metaphor where the aid of Allāh, His carefully tending to a person's affairs, and the speed with which He meets his need has been likened to someone who sits before him, preserves him and tends to him.

"When you" intend to *"ask, ask Allāh,"* alone. The treasures of all providence are with Him, none can grant or withhold save Him. Allāh, Most High, says,

وَسْـَٔلُوا۟ ٱللَّهَ مِن فَضْلِهِۦٓ

"...ask Allāh for His bounty."[5]

The ḥadīth states, "Allāh is angry at whoever does not ask of

[5] *al-Nisā'* (4): 32

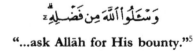

Him."[6] Another ḥadīth mentions, "Each of you must ask his Lord for all his needs, even the strap of his sandal should it break."[7] It is reported that Allāh, Most High, said to Mūsā, peace and blessings be on him and our Prophet, "Mūsā, ask of Me in your supplication - or your prayer - even if it be salt for your dough."

In all affairs, a person must rely on his Master since none can withhold His grant and none can give what He withholds. The servant must not depend on anyone besides Him. A person could fall into the chasm of neglect and become heedless of this reality as a result of which his heart will incline towards creation. The more it does this, the further it will get from his Master because of the weakness of certitude. On the other hand, those who have actualised reliance and certainty turn away from any besides Him and place all their needs at the threshold of His generosity and munificence. He will tend to those who place their reliance in Him. Allāh, Most High, says,

وَمَن يَتَوَكَّلْ عَلَى ٱللَّهِ فَهُوَ حَسْبُهُۥٓ

"Whoever puts his trust in Allāh, He will be enough for him."[8]

---

[6] Aḥmad #9701, Tirmidhī #3373, ibn Mājah #3827 on the authority of Abū Hurayrah.

Its isnād was ruled ḍaʿīf by Dhahabī, *al-Mīzān*, vol. 4, pg. 538 and Arna'ūṭ et. al. However the ḥadīth was ruled ḥasan due to supports by Albānī, *al-Ṣaḥīḥah* #2654

[7] Tirmidhī #3682 on the authority of Anas and he said it was gharīb.

It was declared ḍaʿīf by Albānī, *al-Ḍaʿīfah* #1362

[8] *al-Ṭalāq* (65): 3

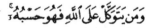

"When you seek aid," when you ask for help in any matter, *"turn to Allāh,"* alone. You know that Allāh, Glorious is He, is omnipotent and everything else is weak and feeble, so much so that it cannot even bring about benefit for itself or repress harm from itself.[9] Help is sought from someone who has the ability to furnish aid, as for one who is *"a burden on his master,"*[10] unable to carry out what he wants for himself let alone anyone else, how can such a one warrant being asked?

Therefore, only Allāh's aid should be sought, and this is seen in His saying,

وَإِيَّاكَ نَسْتَعِينُ ﴿٥﴾

"You alone we ask for help."[11]

In this verse, the object of the verb, asking for help, has been brought before the verb and this is a tool used to express confinement of the meaning to that object.

Whoever is aided by his Master is truly aided, and whoever is forsaken by Him is truly forsaken. al-Ḥasan wrote to 'Umar ibn 'Abdu'l-'Azīz, 'Do not seek the aid of any besides Allāh or Allāh may leave you to him.'

In all affairs and all circumstances, he (ﷺ) directed us to turn

---

[9] The author, *Dalīl al-Fāliḥīn*, vol. 1, pg. 166 adds, 'This is why the statement, *Lā ḥawla wa lā quwwata illā bi'llāh* is one of the treasures of Paradise since it involves the servant absolving his self of might or motion.'

[10] *al-Naḥl* (16): 76

[11] *al-Fātiḥah* (1): 5

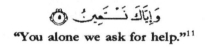

away from others and to direct ourselves to the Master and to trust in Him. He (ﷺ) emphasised the importance of reliance with his words, *"Know that if the nation came together in order to benefit you with something, they would not be able to do so except with something that Allāh has decreed for you..."*

Allāh, Most High, says,

وَإِن يَمْسَسْكَ ٱللَّهُ بِضُرٍّ فَلَا كَاشِفَ لَهُۥٓ إِلَّا هُوَ ۖ وَإِن
يُرِدْكَ بِخَيْرٍ فَلَا رَآدَّ لِفَضْلِهِۦ ۚ

> **"If Allāh afflicts you with harm, no one can remove it except Him. If He desires good for you, no one can avert His favour."**[12]

What is meant is that one must single out Allāh alone in that He is the one who grants benefit or causes harm: none shares with Him in this. It is established that all afflictions and difficulties that creation will face are in His hand to either dispense or withhold. If anyone else wishes to harm you with something He has not decreed, Allāh will divert it away from you by distracting that person from his goal, rendering him incapable of enacting it. He could make him sick, for example, or cause him to forget, or cause his heart to turn away, or He could prevent the actual thing from taking effect by breaking his bow, for example, or causing the arrow to misfire.

This sentence emphasises the need for faith in the divine decree - the good and bad thereof, and it stresses that only He can

[12] *Yūnus* (10): 107

grant benefit or cause harm. It highlights the fact that the true cause in creation is Allāh and that no other has a real impact on what happens or what does not, and that therefore one needs to turn away from any other. Whoever has certain belief in this will only ever see harm or benefit as coming from his Master and as such will only ever petition Him for his need. We take refuge with Allāh from believing that any object of creation can procure benefit or cause harm for that is minor *shirk*, rather it is obvious that it is major *shirk*.

"Allāh has decreed for you... Allāh has decreed against you," is in full conformity to his (ﷺ) teaching that a persons' provision, lifespan, deeds, and whether he is felicitous or wretched have already been recorded.

"The Pens have been lifted," i.e. they have been put aside and writing has ceased, having been completed. All that is and will be has been recorded and cannot now be altered. *"And the scrolls"* upon which the decrees are transcribed such as the Preserved Tablet *"have dried,"* and as such are complete since the ink of a scroll that is still being written on is moist, or at least some of it. There can be no revision, no alteration and no abrogation. This phrase is then a metonym referring to the *a-priori* recording of decrees and their completion. This is an excellent metonym, concise in wording and increases the sense of gravity of what is being said. The Book and Sunnah prove this fact and anyone who knows this and witnesses it with his heart will find trusting in his Master and turning away from any besides Him easy.

If one were to suppose that this narration contradicts the saying of Allāh,

يَمۡحُواْ ٱللَّهُ مَا يَشَآءُ وَيُثۡبِتُۖ وَعِندَهُۥٓ أُمُّ ٱلۡكِتَٰبِ ﴿٣٩﴾

"Allāh erases what He wills or endorses it. The Master Copy of the Book is in His hands."[13]

we would say that this is not the case since the erasure and endorsement is something that itself has been recorded and is done with; this is because the decree is of two types: irrevocable and conditional.

"This was narrated to us in Tirmidhī," one of the researching scholars said this ḥadīth was recorded by a group of people via numerous routes to ibn 'Abbās. The fact that ibn 'Abbās was given this advice has also been recorded from 'Alī, Abū Sa'īd, Sahl ibn Sa'd and 'Abdullāh ibn Ja'far but all of their isnāds contain weakness. Ibn Mandah and others said that the most authentic chain was the one recorded by Tirmidhī. *"And he said it was ḥasan ṣaḥīḥ,"* Sakhāwī, *Takhrīj al-Arba'īn* said the isnād was ḥasan and explained why. Then he said, 'In summary, the ḥadīth is established via the ḥadīth of Laylah and the others already mentioned. This is why Ḍiyā' placed it in his *Mukhtārah*, indeed it was ruled ṣaḥīḥ by 'Irāqī, *al-Amālī*, following Tirmidhī. Ibn Mandah said that its isnād was famous and its narrators trustworthy and precise.'[14]

"Another narration, not in Tirmidhī," rather in 'Abd ibn Ḥumayd with a ḍa'īf isnād. Aḥmad records it with two isnāds that are munqaṭi' with the words,

"Young lad, should I not teach you some words

[13] *al-Ra'd* (13): 39

[14] These words are taken from author's, *Dalīl al-Fāliḥīn*, vol. 1, pg. 65

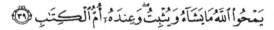

> through which Allāh will occasion benefit for you?" I said, "Of course!" He said, "Safeguard Allāh and He will safeguard you. Safeguard Allāh and you will find Him in front of you. Know Allāh in times of ease and He will know you in times of hardship. When you ask, ask Allāh. When you seek aid, turn to Allāh. The Pen has dried (after having written) all that will occur. If the whole of creation, in its entirety, was to try and effectuate some benefit for you through something that Allāh has not ordained, they would not be able to do so; and if they wished to harm you through something that Allāh has not decreed, they would not be able to do so. Know that great good lies in bearing with patience what you dislike, that victory comes with patience, that relief comes with distress, and that with hardship comes ease.'"[15]

The wording of this narration is more complete than the one alluded to by the author above.

"Know Allāh," knowledge is the route to love so the meaning is endear yourself to Allāh, Glorious is He, by adhering resolutely to obedience and avoiding opposing Him, *"in times of ease"* and well-being *"and He will know you in times of hardship,"* assisting you by relieving you of it. He will relieve you of every adversity and provide a way out from every worry and distress by virtue of your having known Him in times of ease. An example of this can be seen in the ḥadīth of the three who were trapped in the cave, the explanation to which has already preceded.

It is also said that the governing words have been omitted from the sentence, so the meaning would be, "Make yourself *known* to

[15] Aḥmad #2803 and it is ṣaḥīḥ

the Angels of *Allāh in times of ease* through adhering resolutely to obedience and worship and *He will know you in times of adversity* through their intercession for your relief and succour." This explanation is proven by the ḥadīth that mentions that if a person is given to supplicating at times of ease, and then supplicates at a time of adversity, the angels will say, 'Lord, this is a familiar voice.' If he does not supplicate at times of ease and then supplicates at a time of adversity, they will say, 'Lord, this is an unfamiliar voice.'[16] However this is a problematic explanation and the ḥadīth, assuming that it is authentic, does not really support this view. The first explanation given above is more befitting.

Point of benefit: the servant's knowing is general and specific, and Allāh's knowing is also general and specific. The general, from the point of view of the servant, is to accept His oneness, Glorious is He, and His lordship, and to have faith in Him. The specific is to devote oneself exclusively to Him and to take comfort and solace with Him, to take delight in His remembrance, to be shy before Him, and to witness Him on all occasions. The general, from the point of view of Allāh, is His all-encompassing knowledge of His servants and His seeing what they hide and what they conceal. The specific is His loving His servant, bringing him close, responding to his supplication and relieving him of adversity. Only those who have attained knowledge in the specific sense will attain His knowledge in the specific sense.

Next is mentioned the core and substance of this advice, *"Know that what missed you,"* and never reached you as per the decree *"could never have afflicted you"* since it was decreed for another *"and what afflicted you"* as per the decree *"could never have missed you,"*

[16] Ibn Rajab has quoted this as a statement of Salmān al-Farisī on pg. 29

since it was decreed to come to you. Only that which is decreed will come to a person. The meaning is that all that will afflict or miss a person, be it good or bad, has already been decided. The ḥadīth recorded by Aḥmad mentions, "Everything has a reality and the servant will not attain the reality of faith until he knows that what afflicted him would never have missed him, and what missed him would never have afflicted him."[17]

This then contains an encouragement towards relegating ones affairs to Allāh and relying on Him, Glorious is He. It teaches us to negate might and motion from all besides Him while witnessing that He does what He wills and knowing that it is not possible to go beyond what He has decreed. This, then is like His saying,

مَآ أَصَابَ
مِن مُّصِيبَةٍ فِى ٱلْأَرْضِ وَلَا فِىٓ أَنفُسِكُمْ إِلَّا فِى كِتَٰبٍ
مِّن قَبْلِ أَن نَّبْرَأَهَآ ۚ إِنَّ ذَٰلِكَ عَلَى ٱللَّهِ يَسِيرٌ ﴿٢٢﴾ لِّكَيْلَا
تَأْسَوْا۟ عَلَىٰ مَا فَاتَكُمْ وَلَا تَفْرَحُوا۟ بِمَآ ءَاتَىٰكُمْ ۗ

"Nothing occurs, either in the earth or in your selves, without its being in a Book before We make it happen. That is so that you will not be grieved about the things that pass you by or exult about the things that come to you."[18]

---

[17] Aḥmad #27490, ibn Abī 'Āṣim #246.
It was ruled ḥasan by Suyūṭī, *al-Jāmi'* #2417 and Wadi'ī, *Ṣaḥīḥ al-Musnad* #1050. Albānī, *Ẓilāl al-Jannah* #246, *al-Ṣaḥīḥah* #2471 ruled it ṣaḥīḥ due to supporting witnesses.

[18] *al-Ḥadīd* (57): 22-23

We asserted that this phrase is the core of this advice because both the preceding and ensuing phrases are based on it and branch off from it. Whoever believes the subject matter of this phrase will have certainty that Allāh is the one who gives benefit and causes harm, and that He is the one who grants and withholds, as such he will obey Him alone, he will safeguard His limits, he will fear Him, hope in Him, love Him, and place obedience to Him before obedience to the created. He will ask Him alone for aid, he will petition Him, he will humbly entreat Him, he will be content with His ordainment in times of hardship and ease, and in cases of grant and withholding.

"Know that victory comes with patience," once a person realises that his life is being lived in accordance to His decree, he (ﷺ) informed us that man, especially the righteous, will accordingly encounter blessings and calamities, and ease and hardship and that, if he is unable to be content, he must adorn himself with patience in the face of any ordainment he finds bitter and that, moreover, he should await Allāh's promise. Allāh has promised that such a person will receive the blessings and mercy of Allāh and that he will guided aright. Tirmidhī records that the Prophet (ﷺ) said, "When Allāh loves a people, He tries them. Whoever is content will have good-pleasure, and whoever is displeased will have displeasure."[19]

---

[19] Tirmidhī #2396, ibn Mājah #4031.

Tirmidhī said that it was ḥasan gharīb. Mundhirī, *al-Targhīb*, vol. 4, pg. 233 said the isnād was ḥasan or ṣaḥīḥ. Ibn Mufliḥ, *al-Ādāb al-Shar'iyyah*, vol. 2, pg. 181 said that the isnād was jayyid. It was ruled ḥasan by Albānī, *al-Ṣaḥīḥah* #146

Aḥmad #23623-23633-23641 records a similar ḥadīth on the authority of Maḥmūd ibn Labīd with the words, "When Allāh loves a people, He tries them. Whoever is patient, for him is patience and whoever despairs, for him is despair." Arna'ūṭ said that the isnād was jayyid.

"Know that victory comes with patience," i.e. victory against the enemies, both the physical and metaphysical, only comes about through steadfastly obeying the Master and steadfastly avoiding disobedience to Him. As such patience is the route to victory. Allāh, Most High, says,

وَٱصْبِرُوٓا۟ ۚ إِنَّ ٱللَّهَ مَعَ ٱلصَّٰبِرِينَ ﴿٤٦﴾

"And be patient, Allāh is with the patient."[20]

i.e. He is with them by aiding them. Therefore the statement induces a person to trust his Master and to disclaim might and motion for himself. The predominate case of a person who relies on himself for aid is that he is not aided; the predominate case of a person who is patient and content with Allāh's knowledge and judgement is that victory is precipitated. His generosity and providence is well recognised.

"That relief comes with distress," that strikes at the very soul. At such a time, relief is swift in coming. Anyone who is in such a state should be patient, expectant of reward, hoping for swift relief, and at all times having a good opinion of his Master. He is the Most Merciful of all those who are merciful, even one's own parents.

The ḥadīth shows that trials are a cause of divine grace as is proven by the statement, *"and that with hardship comes ease."* At times of adversity a person comes to know the magnificence of Allāh and at times of grace a person comes to know the beauty of Allāh. One person said, 'When He confers a blessing on you,

[20] *al-Anfāl* (8): 46

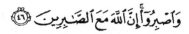

witness His generosity, and when He withholds something from you, witness His overwhelming might. In every circumstance He is tending to you, showering you with His providential care.'

"And that with hardship comes ease," i.e. facilitation. A state of richness is called *yasār*, ease and prosperity, because matters are facilitated therein. The opposite of *yusr*, ease, is *'usr*, hardship. This statement occurs as a verse in the Qur'ān which is repeated twice to show that every hardship is accompanied with two eases. It is reported that he (ﷺ) said, "One hardship will never overcome two eases.'"[21] This is also reported from a group of Companions and is based on the fact that the word ease is an indefinite noun in both instances so as to aggrandise it. As such the second occurrence does not refer to the exact same thing as the first occurrence in keeping with an established linguistic rule. Hardship, on the other hand, is a definite noun in both occurrences, to refer to something familiar, *'ahd*, or the genus of something, *jins*, therefore both instances refer to one and the same thing. This was how Zamakhsharī explained it.

A wonderful wisdom in attaching the onset of relief to intense distress and ease to hardship is that in such circumstances a per-

---

[21] Ṭabarī, Bayhaqī, *Shu'ab* #10013, Ḥākim #3950 and Dhahabī said it was mursal as did Zayla'ī, *Takhrīj al-Kashshāf*, vol. 4, pg. 235. Ibn Ḥajr, *al-Kāfi*, pg. 319 said that it was mursal and that the mawṣūl version was ḍa'īf, in *Taghlīq al-Ta'līq*, vol. 4, pg. 372 he adds that the isnād to al-Ḥasan is ṣaḥīḥ. Albānī, *al-Ḍa'īfah* #4342 said that it was ḍa'īf.

Ibn Abī Ḥātim #19396 records it as a saying of al-Ḥasan.

Ibn Kathīr said, 'The meaning of these words is that in both occurrences, the word *difficulty* is appended to the definite article, *al*, as such it is singular. The word *ease* is left indefinite; as such there is more than one occurrence of it. Therefore the second reference to *difficulty* denotes the same as in the first reference, whereas there is more than one instance of *ease*.'

son gives up hope in any object of creation relieving him. Instead the person turns to Allāh and depends on Him alone. This is the core and essence of *tawakkul*, Allāh, Most High, says,

وَمَن يَتَوَكَّلْ عَلَى ٱللَّهِ فَهُوَ حَسْبُهُۥٓ

"Whoever puts his trust in Allāh, He will be enough for him."[22]

Finally the hardship that has been mentioned in the ḥadīth is not the same as the hardship mentioned in the verse,

يُرِيدُ ٱللَّهُ بِكُمُ ٱلْيُسْرَ وَلَا يُرِيدُ بِكُمُ ٱلْعُسْرَ

"Allāh desires ease for you; He does not desire difficulty for you."[23]

The difficulty talked about in this ḥadīth deals with the vicissitudes of one's worldly life, and the difficulty talked about in the verse is the injunction of rules and regulations that are beyond man's ability to bear. Allāh, Most High, says,

وَمَا جَعَلَ عَلَيْكُمْ فِي ٱلدِّينِ مِنْ حَرَجٍ

"He has not placed any constraint upon you in the religion."[24]

[22] *al-Ṭalāq* (65): 3

[23] *al-Baqarah* (2): 185

[24] *al-Ḥajj* (22): 78

The usage of the word *maʿa*, with, in the previous three sentences is meant literally since the final stages of patience, distress and hardship are the first stages of victory, relief and ease.

In conclusion, this is a great ḥadīth, a central foundation in tending to the rights of Allāh, Most High, relegating oneself to His judgement, witnessing His *Tawḥīd*, and highlighting mankind's innate inability and dire need of Him. When seen in this light, one could justifiably say that this ḥadīth constitutes one half of the religion, indeed all of it. This is because the legal laws either deal with Allāh or other than Him and this ḥadīth deals with all that is connected to Allāh explicitly and to all that is connected to others implicitly. In fact, both are understood from the statement, *"Safeguard Allāh and He will safeguard you."* A whole treatise has been devoted to explaining this ḥadīth.[25]

[25] Perhaps the author is referring to ibn Rajab's monograph.

APPENDIX SIX

Ibn 'Uthaymīn's Commentary

Imām Nawawī, *Riyāḍ al-Ṣāliḥin* #62 records:

> On the authority of ibn 'Abbās (*raḍiyAllāhu 'anhumā*) who said, 'I was sitting behind the Prophet (ﷺ) when he said, "Young lad, I will teach you some words: Safeguard Allāh and He will safeguard you. Safeguard Allāh and you will find Him before you. When you ask, ask Allāh. When you seek aid, turn to Allāh. Know that if the nation came together in order to benefit you with something, they would not be able to do so except with something that Allāh has decreed for you; and were they to come together in order to harm you with something, they would not be able to do so except with something that Allāh has decreed against you. The Pens have been lifted and the scrolls have dried."[1]

This was narrated to us in Tirmidhī and he said it was ḥasan ṣaḥīḥ. Another narration, not in Tirmidhī, has, "Safeguard Allāh and you will find Him in front of

[1] Tirmidhī #2516 who said it was ḥasan ṣaḥīḥ

> you. Know Allāh in times of ease and He will know you in times of hardship. Know that what missed you could never have afflicted you and what afflicted you could never have missed you." It concludes with the words, "Know that victory comes with patience, that relief comes with distress, and that with hardship comes ease."

Ibn 'Uthaymīn, *Sharḥ Riyāḍ al-Ṣāliḥin*, vol. 1, pp. 332-337, said:

"I was sitting behind the Prophet (ﷺ)," riding with him.

"Young lad," since ibn 'Abbās, at that time, was still a boy. When the Prophet (ﷺ) passed away he had just attained the age of puberty, i.e. around the age of fifteen, sixteen or less.

"Safeguard Allāh and He will safeguard you," this is a magnificent pronouncement and of paramount importance. *"Safeguard Allāh,"* through upkeeping His law and religion by enacting what He has commanded and avoiding what He has prohibited. This is also done by learning all that you need to perform your acts of worship and carry out your social dealings and trade. The knowledge learned would also be employed to call people to Allāh, Mighty and Magnificent. All of these are examples of safeguarding Allāh.

Allāh Himself stands in no need whatsoever of anyone, He does not need anyone to safeguard Him, and this is why the meaning of this sentence is safeguarding His religion. In the same way, Allāh, Most High, says,

يَٰٓأَيُّهَا ٱلَّذِينَ
ءَامَنُوٓاْ إِن تَنصُرُواْ ٱللَّهَ يَنصُرۡكُمۡ وَيُثَبِّتۡ أَقۡدَامَكُمۡ ٧

"You who have faith! If you help Allāh, He will help you and make your feet firm."[2]

One must not suppose that a person can actually help Allāh Himself because Allāh is Self-Sufficient and Rich, beyond any need. This is why He says in another verse,

ذَٰلِكَ وَلَوۡ يَشَآءُ ٱللَّهُ لَٱنتَصَرَ مِنۡهُمۡ

"That is how it is to be. If Allāh had willed, He could avenge Himself on them."[3]

Mankind cannot withstand Him,

وَمَا كَانَ ٱللَّهُ لِيُعۡجِزَهُۥ مِن شَيۡءٖ
فِي ٱلسَّمَٰوَٰتِ وَلَا فِي ٱلۡأَرۡضِۚ إِنَّهُۥ كَانَ عَلِيمٗا قَدِيرٗا ٤٤

"Allāh cannot be withstood in any way, either in the heavens or on earth. He is All-Knowing, All-Powerful."[4]

Therefore this sentence proves that whoever safeguards Allāh, Allāh will safeguard him. He will safeguard His body, his wealth, his family and his religion; the latter being the most important.

---

[2] *Muhammad* (47): 7

[3] *Muhammad* (47): 4

[4] *Fāṭir* (35): 44

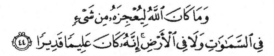

He will secure you from wandering astray and falling into misguidance. Each time a person seeks guidance, Allāh will increase him in it,

وَالَّذِينَ اهْتَدَوْا زَادَهُمْ هُدًى وَءَاتَىٰهُمْ تَقْوَىٰهُمْ ﴿١٧﴾

"He increases in guidance those who are already guided and gives them their *taqwā*."[5]

Each time a person takes the path to misguidance, and refuge is sought with Allāh, Allāh will increase his misguidance as mentioned in the ḥadīth, "When a person commits a sin, a black spot appears on his heart. If he repents, it is wiped away..."[6] but if the person keeps sinning, the black spot will increase until it covers the heart and seals it. We ask Allāh for well-being!

Therefore, He will safeguard your religion, your body, your wealth and your family.

"Safeguard Allāh and you will find Him before you," another wording has, *"in front of you."* Safeguard Allāh in the way previously mentioned and you will find Him before you and in front of you: the meaning is one and the same: you will find Allāh guiding you to all good and curbing all evil from you, this is especially true if you safeguard Allāh by seeking His aid for when a person asks

---

[5] *Muḥammad* (47): 17

[6] Tirmidhī #3334 who said it was ḥasan ṣaḥīḥ and ibn Mājah #4244 on the authority of Abū Hurayrah.

Ibn Taymiyyah, *Majmū'*, vol. 14, pg. 48 said it was ṣaḥīḥ. Albānī, *Ṣaḥīḥ al-Targhīb* #3141 said it was ḥasan.

cf. Muslim #144 on the authority of Hudhayfah.

Allāh for aid and puts his trust in Him, Allāh will suffice him. Whoever is in this position will stand in no need of any besides Allāh. Allāh, Most High, says,

يَٰٓأَيُّهَا ٱلنَّبِيُّ حَسۡبُكَ ٱللَّهُ وَمَنِ ٱتَّبَعَكَ مِنَ ٱلۡمُؤۡمِنِينَ ٦٤

> **"O Prophet! Allāh is enough for you and for the believers who follow you."[7]**

وَإِن يُرِيدُوٓاْ أَن يَخۡدَعُوكَ فَإِنَّ حَسۡبَكَ ٱللَّهُۚ

> **"If they intend to deceive you, Allāh is enough for you."[8]**

If Allāh is enough for a person, i.e. suffices him, no evil will befall him.

"When you ask, ask Allāh. When you seek aid, turn to Allāh," i.e. do not depend on created beings. A person who is poor, having no money, should ask Allāh for sustenance and he will find it coming to him via routes he could never have imagined! If, on the other hand, he were to beg of people he may or may not get what he needs. This is why it is mentioned in a ḥadīth, "One of you taking his rope, gathering firewood, and selling it is better than his begging people: they could give him something or they could refuse."[9]

---

[7] *al-Anfāl* (8): 64

[8] *al-Anfāl* (8): 62

[9] Bukhārī #1470-1480-2074-2374 on the authority of Abū Hurayrah. Bukhārī #1471-2075-2353 on the authority of Zubayr ibn al-'Awwām.

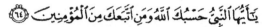

When you ask, ask Allāh: 'O Allāh! Grant me sustenance', 'O Allāh! Make me independent of all save You,' etc. The same applies to asking for aid, ask Him for aid and only ask created beings for aid in cases of dire emergency and even then, know that they are merely a means to an end, do not depend on them, depend instead on Allāh, Mighty and Magnificent.

These two phrases show that asking others besides Allāh is a deficiency in *Tawḥīd* and this is why it is disliked to ask any besides Allāh, be the matter small or large. If Allāh, Glorious is He, wants to aid you, His aid will come to you be it through routes that are obvious to you or hidden from you. Allāh could turn such harm away from you as would have been unbearable, and He could come to your aid through the medium of one of His creation. In the latter case it is not permissible for you to forget that Allāh, Mighty and Magnificent, was the true source of help.

Today you find some of the ignorant venerating the disbelievers and respecting them greatly because, on the face of it, they came to the aid of their country when requested. They fail to realise that the disbelievers are their enemies and they have, more often than not, ulterior motives in helping them. They are your enemies until the Day of Rising; it is not permissible for anyone to take them as close friends and protectors, or to help them or to supplicate for them. We have even heard some of the ignoramuses declaring their intentions to slaughter animals for the sake of disbelievers, and refuge is sought with Allāh! You find Muslims naming their children after them and supplicating for them! It was Allāh who caused them to come to your aid, without Him they would not be there. The One who brings benefit or harm is Allāh and it is He who caused them to come to your defence as is mentioned in a ḥadīth, "Allāh would support this religion by an evil person."[10]

We must not forget the grace of Allāh and that it was Him who has caused them to come to our aid, and we must inform the masses of this. When we hear their statements articulating how much they depend on them, and how they themselves came to their aid, it is obligatory for us to explain to them that such attitudes are actually a deficiency in *Tawḥid*. Allāh knows best.

"Know that if the nation came together in order to benefit you with something, they would not be able to do so except with something that Allāh has decreed for you," so when they do actually benefit you with something, you should know that it is from Allāh since He has decreed it for you. The Prophet (ﷺ) did not state that they would not be able to bring you any benefit at all, rather he said that they could not benefit you with something that Allāh has not decreed for you.

Undoubtedly, people can help each other and they can support each other, but only in something that has already been decreed. Therefore, first and foremost, the grace for doing so is from Allāh, Mighty and Magnificent. He is the One who allowed someone to help you, to be good to you or to remove your distress.

The opposite also holds true: man cannot harm you with something unless it has been decreed by Allāh.

True faith in this leads a person to depend on His Lord, to rely on Him alone and not be worried about anyone knowing that

[10] Bukhārī #3062-4203-6606 on the authority of Abū Hurayrah.

only that harm which He has decreed would come his way. As such, he will place his hope in Allāh and stick closely to Him. It is for this reason that, when the Salaf of this nation placed their dependency and reliance in Allāh, they were not harmed by those who plotted against them,

وَإِن تَصْبِرُوا۟ وَتَتَّقُوا۟ لَا يَضُرُّكُمْ كَيْدُهُمْ شَيْـًٔا ۗ
إِنَّ ٱللَّهَ بِمَا يَعْمَلُونَ مُحِيطٌ ﴿١٢٠﴾

> **"If you are patient and have *taqwā*, their scheming will not harm you in any way. Allāh encompasses what they do."[11]**

"The Pens have been lifted and the scrolls have dried," Allāh has completed all that He has decreed, the pens have been taken away and the scrolls are dry, there is no need for revision or change. Whatever afflicts you would never have missed you as is mentioned in the variant wording, *"Know that what afflicted you could never have missed you and what missed you could never have afflicted you."*

"Know" with certainty *"that victory comes with patience,"* so if you are patient and steadfast, doing what Allāh has ordered and you ask Him for victory, He will grant you victory. Patience subsumes patience in obedience to Allāh, patience in avoiding disobedience, and patience in the face of adversity and tribulation.

The enemy attacks from all directions, as a result a person could well despair, think that he is unable to counter him, and give up Jihād. Jihād could become legislated, a person could be injured, despair and give up; he could also continue the fight and receive

[11] *Āli 'Imrān* (3): 120

injury from his enemy, but he must bear it patiently,

إِن يَمْسَسْكُمْ قَرْحٌ فَقَدْ مَسَّ الْقَوْمَ قَرْحٌ مِّثْلُهُ

"If you receive a wound, they have already received a similar wound."[12]

وَلَا تَهِنُوا
فِي ابْتِغَاءِ الْقَوْمِ إِن تَكُونُوا تَأْلَمُونَ فَإِنَّهُمْ يَأْلَمُونَ كَمَا
تَأْلَمُونَ وَتَرْجُونَ مِنَ اللَّهِ مَا لَا يَرْجُونَ

"Do not relax in the pursuit of the enemy. If you feel pain, they too are feeling it just as you are, but you hope for something from Allāh which they cannot hope for."[13]

"That relief comes with distress," whenever something distresses you and that adversity intensifies, know that relief is close. Allāh, Mighty and Magnificent, says in His Book,

أَمَّن يُجِيبُ الْمُضْطَرَّ إِذَا دَعَاهُ
وَيَكْشِفُ السُّوءَ وَيَجْعَلُكُمْ خُلَفَاءَ الْأَرْضِ أَإِلَٰهٌ
مَّعَ اللَّهِ قَلِيلًا مَّا تَذَكَّرُونَ ﴿٦٢﴾

"He who responds to the oppressed when they call on Him and removes their distress, and has appointed you as *khalifs* on the earth. Is there

[12] *Āli 'Imrān* (3): 140

[13] *al-Nisā'* (4): 104

another god besides Allāh? How little you pay heed!"[14]

So when adversity intensifies, know that Allāh's relief is close at hand.

"And that with hardship comes ease," every hardship is followed by ease, rather each hardship is surrounded by two eases, an ease before it and an ease that follows it. Allāh, Most High, says,

فَإِنَّ مَعَ الْعُسْرِ يُسْرًا ﴿٥﴾ إِنَّ مَعَ الْعُسْرِ يُسْرًا ﴿٦﴾

"For truly with hardship comes ease; truly with hardship comes ease."[15]

Ibn 'Abbās said, 'One hardship will never overcome two eases.'

A person should always bear this advice in mind and he should follow what the Prophet (ﷺ) enjoined upon the son of his uncle, 'Abdullāh ibn 'Abbās (*radiyAllāhu 'anhumā*). Allāh is the One who grants accord.

---

[14] *al-Naml* (27): 62

[15] *al-Sharh* (94): 5-6

Index of Sects

Ahlu'l-Kalām: Adherents to speculative theology, people seeking to explain the articles and premises of belief and to give evidences for them based on philosophy and logic.

Bāṭiniyyah: A sect of the Shī'a, the followers of Ismā'īl ibn Ja'far. They were of the belief that the legal texts were merely superficial expressions carrying inner meanings that oppose what is outwardly understood of them, examples lie with their explanations of Paradise, Hell and the Last Day.

Ḥashwiyyah: A term frequently used by the innovators to refer to Ahlu'l-Sunnah, the Ahl'l-Ḥadith, those who affirmed the Attributes of Allāh. The first to use this term was 'Amr ibn 'Ubaid al-Mu'tazilī who said that 'Abdullāh ibn 'Umar bin al-Khaṭṭāb was a Ḥashwī.

Jabariyyah: Followers of the school of Jahm ibn Ṣafwān in his belief that all actions are decreed by Allāh and man has no control over them at all, instead he is forced to do what he does.

Jahmiyyah: Followers of Jahm ibn Ṣafwān in his denial of the Names and Attributes of Allāh.

Karrāmiyyah: Followers of Muḥammad ibn Karrām (d. 255H), they divided into many sub-sects and were famous for their likening of Allāh to His creation (*tashbīh*).

Mutakallimūn: Speculative Theologians, adherents to *kalām*.

Mu'tazila: Followers of Wāṣil ibn 'Aṭā' al-Ghazzāl who abandoned the circles of Ḥasan al-Baṣrī. They negated the Attributes of Allāh for fear of likening Him to His creation, yet affirmed His Names. From amongst their beliefs was that a person who committed a major sin was neither a believer nor a disbeliever, rather of a station between the two stations, but he would be consigned to Hellfire forever. They were from the rank and file of the Mutakallimūn and gave precedence to their intellects over the divine texts.

Qadariyyah: Those who held the belief that man has complete free will in all that he does and that Allāh has no control over him.

Qarāmiṭa: A sect holding the same belief as the Bāṭiniyyah and followers of Maymūn ibn Daysān.

Falāsifa: Those philosophers who promoted the 'wisdom' of the Greeks, the Greek philosophers who did not believe in the Resurrection as it is mentioned in the Book and Sunnah, nor did they affirm the Names and Attributes of Allāh. From amongst their leaders was Aristotle, the student of Plato and from amongst their latter proponents was al-Fārābī and ibn Sīnā.

Index of Arabic Words

Awliyā': plural of *walī*; friend, ally, loyal companion. From the word *wilāyah* meaning loyalty and closeness, the opposite of enmity.

'Ayy: withholding the tongue from speaking, carefully considering each word before it is said.

Barzakh: barrier, isthmus, A barrier that is erected between the deceased and this life preventing him from returning and a generic reference to the life that commences after death.

Bayān: Speech, clarification, discourse. It is of two types: the first whereby the intended meaning is expressed clearly, whatever language it may be in, this category is not regarded as magic; the second whereby the intended meaning is expressed in eloquent, cleverly doctored phrases based upon specific rules such that one listening takes pleasure in hearing the words and they affect his very heart. This category is what has been likened to magic as it captivates and beguiles the heart and overcomes the soul to the point that the face of reality could be transformed to illusion and the one captivated perceive only that which the speaker wants him to perceive. This category can be used in a commendable fashion and in a blameworthy fashion. As for the commendable form, it is to direct the person towards the truth and use these methods to aid the truth. As for the blameworthy form, it is to direct the person towards falsehood or envelop him in confusion such that the truth is seen as falsehood and falsehood as truth. This is completely blameworthy and has been likened to that which is completely blameworthy - magic

Bid'ah: innovation, that which is newly introduced into the religion of Allāh.

Ḍa'īf: weak; the ḥadīth that is neither ṣaḥīḥ nor ḥasan because it fails to meet one of their requirements. It is of varying degrees of severity, the most severe of which being mawḍū', fabricated.

Dhawq: taste, perceptivity, technically referring to spiritual experience, *dhawq* is a more temporary state of *wajd.* One may receive some forms of inspiration in the heart as a result of these states however this inspiration should always be compared to the Book and Sunnah to ascertain its correctness.

Dhikr: remembrance, recollection, technically referring the remembrance of Allāh.

Du'ā: supplication, invocation, it is an action of worship that may only be directed to Allāh. It is of two types, supplication through worship (*du'ā 'ibādah*) and supplication of request (*du'ā mas'alah*). The first type of *du'ā* can be understood when one understands that every act of worship is done with the unstated plea that Allāh accept that action of worship and the desire to draw closer to him; and hence attain His pleasure. Hence every action of worship is a type of request to Allāh. The second type of *du'ā* is whereby one explicitly asks his Lord of something such as 'O Allāh! Grant me good in this world and the Hereafter.' The second type includes the first type and the first type necessitates the second type.

Ḥadīth: A text attributed to the Prophet (ﷺ) describing his actions, words, descriptions and tacit approvals. It consists of two portions, the body of the text (*matn*) and the *isnād*. Rarely the term is also used to refer to a text attributed to a Companion or a *Tābi'ī*.

Ḥāfiẓ: pl. *ḥuffāẓ*. Ḥadīth Master, commonly referred to one who has memorised at least 100,000 ḥadīths.

Ḥasan: good, fair. A ḥadīth whose *isnād* is continuously linked of just, morally upright narrators but whose precision (*ḍabṭ*) falls short of the requirements of the ṣaḥīḥ ḥadīth; containing no irregularity (*shādh*) and no hidden defect (*'illah*). A ḥadīth can be ḥasan in and of itself, or contain a defect but still be ruled to be so due to supporting evidences.

Ḥayā': modesty, derived from the word *ḥayāt*, or life because it is through modesty that the heart is granted life and it is through the absence of modesty that it dies. It is a state that arises through the servant being aware that Allāh is watching him, having love, fear and awe of Him and thinking little of himself. Al-Junayd said, '*al-Ḥayā'*' is to recognise the bounties of Allāh and then to recognise ones own shortcomings. Through this a state is engendered which is termed *al-Ḥayā'*, the reality of which is that it is a mannerism that prevents one from committing vile actions and from being lax in fulfilling the rights of Allāh.'

Ḥudūd: limits, boundaries. The limits ordained by Allāh, prescribed punishments.

Ḥulūl wa-l-Ittiḥād: incarnation and unification, the settling of a superior faculty upon a support.

Iḥsān: beneficence, excellence. To worship Allāh as if one is seeing Him, and knowing that even though one sees Him not, He sees the servant.

Ikhlāṣ: sincerity, to strip oneself of worshiping any besides Allāh such that everything one does is performed only to draw closer to Him and for His pleasure. It is to purify ones actions from any but the Creator having a share in them, from any defect or self-desire. The one who has true *ikhlāṣ* (*mukhliṣ*) will be free of *riyā'*.

'Ilm: knowledge.

Īmān: The firm belief, complete acknowledgement and acceptance of all that Allāh and His Messenger have commanded to have faith in, submitting to it both inwardly and outwardly. It is the acceptance and belief of the heart that includes the actions of the heart and body, therefore it encompasses the establishment of the whole religion. This is why the Imāms and Salaf used to say, 'Faith is the statement of the heart and tongue, action of the heart, tongue and limbs.' Hence it comprises statement, action and belief, it increases through obedience and decreases through disobedience. It includes the beliefs of faith, its morals and manners and the actions demanded by it.

Islām: submission, submitting to the will of Allāh through following His law as revealed upon the tongue of the Messenger (ﷺ).

Isnād: support. The chain of authorities on which a narration is based, linking the end narrator of a narration to the one it is attributed to, be it the Prophet (ﷺ) or anyone else, narrator by narrator.

Istidrāj: gradually leading to a desired conclusion. Technically refers to Allāh gradually leading one who displays ingratitude to His favours to his destruction as a befitting recompense. Some of the Salaf would say, 'When you see Allāh bestowing His blessings upon you, one after the other, and you are steadfast in disobeying Him, then beware for this is *istidrāj* by which He gradually leads you to destruction.'

Ittibā': following, technically referring to following the Sunnah of the Prophet (ﷺ).

'Iyāfah: the practice of divination through frightening birds, the sounds they make and the directions in which they fly.

Jāhiliyyah: Pre-Islāmic Ignorance. Technically this refers to the condition of a people before the guidance of Allāh reaches them, or the state of a people that prevents them from accepting the guidance of Allāh.

Jahl: ignorance.

Kalām: speech, discourse. Technically used to refer to dialectics and scholastic theology.

Kufr: denial, rejection, hiding, technically referring to disbelief. It can be major (removing a person from the fold of Islām) or minor (not removing a person from the fold of Islām).

Majhūl: unknown. A reference to a narrator from whom only one narrator narrates (*majhūl al-ʿain*) or whose state of precision (*ḍabṭ*) is unknown (*majhūl al-ḥāl*), such a narrator makes the *isnād ḍaʿīf.*

Maʿrifah: gnosis. Knowledge that is acted upon by the one who knows, the Gnostic of Allāh is one who has knowledge of Allāh, the path that leads to Allāh and the pitfalls of that path. He is one who knows Allāh, His Names, Attributes and Actions and then displays *ṣidq* and *ikhlāṣ* towards Allāh in all things. He works towards removing all despicable morals and mannerisms and has *ṣabr* in all of this.

Matrūk: abandoned. A narrator who is accused of lying, or makes many mistakes, or makes mistakes in aḥādith that are agreed upon, or narrates from famous narrators that which those narrators do not know.

Munqaṭiʿ: that ḥadīth from which the narrator just before the Companion has been omitted from its *isnād.*

Murāqabah: self-inspection. The servant having the sure knowledge that Allāh sees him in all circumstances and knows all that he is doing, as such the he does his utmost not to fall into the prohibited matters and to correct his own failings.

Mursal: disconnected. A ḥadīth whereby a *Tābi'ī* narrates directly from the Prophet (ﷺ) without mentioning the Companion. In the view of the majority of Scholars it is a sub-category of ḍa'īf.

Muṣḥaf: text of the Qur'ān

Qadr: Divine Decree and Destiny.

Qur'ān: The actual Word of Allāh revealed to the Prophet (ﷺ) in the Arabic language through the medium of the Angel Gabriel and the greatest miracle bestowed him. It consists of 114 chapters commencing with al-Fātiḥah and ending with an-Nās.

Riyā': showing off, ostentation, an example of which lies in person beautifying actions of worship because he knows people are watching.

Ruqyā: recitation used to cure an illness or disease. It can only be done in the Arabic tongue, in words whose meaning is understood, using verses of the Qur'ān or supplications of the Prophet combined with the belief that it is only Allāh who in reality gives the cure.

Ṣāḥīḥ: correct, authentic. A ḥadith which has a continuously linked *isnād*, of just, morally upright and precise narrators; containing no irregularity (*shādh*) or hidden defect (*'illah*). Hence five conditions have to be met: the *isnād* being continuously linked;

the justice (*'adl*) of the narrator; the precision (*ḍabṭ*) of the narrator; its not being *shādh*; and its not containing an *'illah*. The ḥadīth can be ṣaḥīḥ in and of itself, or it can contain a defect but still be ruled to be ṣaḥīḥ due to supporting evidences.

Salaf: predecessors. Technically used to refer to the best generations of Muslims, the first three generation: the *Ṣaḥābah*, the *Tābi'ūn* and the *Tab' Tābi'ūn* due to the ḥadīth, "The best of people are my generation, then the one that follows, then the one that follows."

Ṣidq: truthfulness, the conformity of the inner to the outer such that the deeds and statements of the person do not belie his beliefs and vice-versa. *Ṣidq* is the foundation of faith and results in peace of mind, lying is the foundation of hypocrisy and results in doubt and suspicion, and this is why the two can never co-exist without being at odds with each other. al-Junayd was asked as to whether *ṣidq* and *ikhlāṣ* were the same or different and he replied, 'They are different, *ṣidq* is the root and *ikhlāṣ* is the branch. *Ṣidq* is the foundation of everything and *ikhlāṣ* only comes into play once one commences an action. Actions are only acceptable when they combine both.' The one who has true *ṣidq* will be free of self-conceit.

Shādh: irregular, odd. A ḥadīth narrated by a trustworthy and precise narrator that contradicts the narrative of other narrators or the narration of one more trustworthy and precise than him, provided that a reconciliation is not possible.

Shirk: association, technically referring to directing a right that is due to Allāh Alone to another object of creation, either completely or partially. It can be major (removing a person from the fold of Islām) or minor (not removing a person from the fold of Islām).

Sunnah: way, path. The actions, words, descriptions, commands, prohibitions and tacit approvals of the Prophet (ﷺ).

Tābi'ūn: The generation following that of the Companions.

Tab' Tābi'ūn: The generation following that of the *Tābi'ūn.*

Tadlīs: deceit. An action of a narrator whereby he makes out that he heard something from a particular narrator what he did not hear or conceals the identity of the one he is narrating from. In order to do so, he will use terms that are vague such as 'such-and-such said' and 'on the authority of such-and-such.' The first type of *tadlīs* is blameworthy and constitutes a defect in the *isnād.* The second is dependant upon exactly what was done and the motives of the narrator, it can be blameworthy or not.

Taqwā: the basic meaning of which is setting a barrier between two things. This is why it is said that one *ittaqā* with his shield, i.e. he set it as a barrier between him and the one who wished him evil. Therefore it is as if the one who has taqwa (*muttaqi*) has used his following the commands of Allāh and avoiding His prohibitions as a barrier between himself and the Punishment. Hence he has preserved and fortified himself against the punishment of Allāh through his obeying Him.

Ṭarq: the practice of divination through drawing lines in the earth or equally the practice of throwing gravel onto the ground and divination by the shapes subsequently formed therein.

Tawḥīd: unification, monotheism, the belief in the absolute Oneness of Allāh. It is to believe that Allāh Alone is the creator, nourisher, and sustainer of the worlds; it is to believe that Allāh Alone deserves to be worshipped; and it is to believe that He has unique and perfect Names and Attributes that far transcend anything that one can imagine.

Ṭiyarah: seeing bad omens in things.

Waḥdatu-l-Wujūd: The unity of existence, the heretical belief that Allāh is everywhere and everything.

Wajd: strong emotion, technically referring to spiritual ecstasy. The heart experiencing sudden surges of intense love, desire, awe and glorification of Allāh.

Wara': pious caution, scrupulousness. A mannerism through which the heart is purified of all that would sully it and has been excellently summarised in the saying of the Prophet (ﷺ), "From the excellence of ones Islām is his leaving that which does not concern him." It is to leave all that causes one doubt, all that does not concern him, to continuously bring oneself to account and to devote oneself to Allāh. Some of the Salaf said, 'None attains the reality of *taqwā* until he leaves that which is harmless for fear of falling into that which is harmful.'

Yaqīn: certainty. It is to faith (*Īmān*) what the soul is to the body, it is the soul to the actions of the heart which in turn formulate the souls to the actions of the limbs and through it one attains the rank of Ṣiddīq. From *yaqīn* does *tawakkul* (absolute reliance in Allāh) sprout and through *yaqīn* is all doubt, suspicion and worry dispelled and the heart filled with love, hope and fear of Allāh. *Yaqīn* is of three levels, that which arises from knowledge (*'ilm al-yaqīn*), seeing (*'ain al-yaqīn*) and actual experience (*ḥaqq al-yaqīn*).

Translators Bibliography

al-Ājurrī, Abū Bakr Muḥammad ibn al-Ḥusayn

al-Sharī'ah [Dār al-Waṭan, Riyadh, 1st ed. 1997/1418, notes by 'Abdullāh ibn Sulaymān, 5+1 vols]

Ṣifātu-l-Ghurabā' [Dār al-Khulafā' li-l-Kitāb al-Islāmī, 2nd ed., with the notes of Badr ibn 'Abdullāh al-Badr]

al-Albānī, Muḥammad Nāṣir ad-Dīn,

Ḍa'īf Abū Dāwūd [al-Maktab al-Islāmī, Beirūt, 1st ed. 1991/1412]

Ḍa'īf ibn Mājah [al-Maktab al-Islāmī, Beirūt, 1st ed. 1988/1408]

Ḍa'īf al-Jāmi' as-Ṣaghīr [al-Maktab al-Islāmī, Beir˜t, 3rd ed. 1990/1410]

Ḍa'īf at-Targhīb wa-t-Tarhīb [Maktabah al-Ma'ārif, Riyādh, 1st ed. 2000/1421, 2 vols]

'ilāl al-Jannah [al-Maktab al-Islāmī, Beirūt, 2nd ed. 1985/1405]

Ghāyatu-l-Marām [al-Maktab al-Islāmī, Beirūt, 4th ed. 1994/1414]

Irwā' al-Ghalīl [al-Maktab al-Islāmī, Beirūt, 2nd ed. 1985/1405, 8+1 vols.]

Ṣaḥīḥ Abū Dāwūd [al-Maktab al-Islāmī, Beirūt, 1st ed. 1989/1409, 3 vols.]

Ṣaḥīḥ Adab al-Mufrad [Dār as-Ṣiddīq, al-Jubayl, 2nd ed. 1994/

1415]

Ṣaḥīḥ ibn Mājah [al-Maktab al-Islāmī, Beirūt, 1st ed. 1986/ 1407, 2 vols.]

Ṣaḥīḥ al-Jāmiʿ as-Ṣaghīr [al-Maktab al-Islāmī, Beirūt, 3rd ed. 1988/1408, 2 vols.]

Ṣaḥīḥ at-Tirmidhī [al-Maktab al-Islāmī, Beirūt, 1st ed. 1988/ 1408, 3 vols.]

Ṣaḥīḥ at-Targhīb wa-t-Tarhīb [Maktabah al-Maʿārif, Riyādh, 1st ed. 2000/1421, 3 vols.]

Silsilah Aḥādīth as-Ṣaḥīḥah [Maktabah al-Maʿārif, Riyādh, 2nd ed. 1986/1407, 10 vols.]

Silsilah Aḥādīth ad-Ḍaʿīfah [Maktabah al-Maʿārif, Riyādh, 5th ed. 1992/1412, 12 vols.]

Tamām al-Minnah [Dār ar-Rāyah, Riyādh, 3rd ed. 1989/1409]

Abu Nuʿaym, Aḥmad ibn ʿAbdullāh al-Aṣfahānī

Ḥilyatu-l-Awliyā' [Dār al-Kutub al-ʿIlmiyyah, Beirut, 1st ed. 1997/1418, notes by Muṭṣaphā ʿAṭā', 12+2 vols.]

al-ʿAdhīmʿAbādī, Abū at-Ṭayyib Muḥammad Shamsu-l-Ḥaqq

ʿAwn al-Maʿbūd Sharḥ Sunan Abū Dawūd [al-Maktabah as-Salafiyyah, Medina, 2nd ed. 1969/1388, in the margin of which is ibn al-Qayyim, *Sharḥ Abū Dāwūd*, 13 vols.]

Aḥmad ibn Ḥanbal

Musnad [Mu'assasah ar-Risālah, Beirut, 1st ed. 1995/1416, notes by Shuʿayb al-Arnaʿūṭ et. al., 45+5 vols.]

al-Baghawī, Abū Muḥammad al-Ḥusayn ibn Masʿūd al-Farā'

Sharḥ as-Sunnah [al-Maktab al-Islāmī, Beir˘t, 2nd ed. 1983/ 1403, notes by Shuʿayb al-Arnaʿūṭ, 15+1 vols.]

al-Bayhaqī, Abū Bakr Aḥmad ibn al-Ḥusayn

Shuʿab al-Īmān [Dār al-Kutub al-ʿIlmiyyah, Beirut, 1st ed. 1990/1410, notes by Muḥammad Zaghlūl, 7+2 vols.]

Dalā'il an-Nubuwwah [Dār al-Kutub al-ʿIlmiyyah, Beirut, 1st ed. 1985/1405, ed. A. Qalʿajī, 6+1 vols.]

Sunan al-Kubrā [Dār al-Fikr, 1st ed. 1996/1416, 15 vols.]

al-Dhahabī, Muḥammad ibn Aḥmad,

Siyar al-A'lām an-Nubulā' [Mu'assasah Risālah, 11th ed. 1996/1417, ed. S. al-Arna'ūt, 23+2 vols.]

Tartīb al-Mawḍū'āt [Dār al-Kutub al-'Ilmiyyah, Beirut, 1st Ed. 1994/1415]

al-Ghazālī, Abū Ḥāmid

Iḥyā' 'Ulūm ad-Dīn [Dār al-Khayr, 4th Ed. 1997/1417, notes by al-'Irāqī, 5 vols.]

al-Ḥākim, Muḥammad ibn 'Abdullāh,

al-Mustadrak 'alā as-Ṣaḥīḥayn [Dār al-Kutub al-'Ilmiyyah, Beirut, 4+1 vols.]

Ibn 'Abdu-l-Barr, Abū 'Umar Yūsuf

Jāmi' al-Bayān al-'Ilm [Dār ibn al-Jawzī, Dammām, 4th ed. 1998/1419, notes by Abū al-Ashbāl az-Zuhayrī, 2 vols]

Tamhīd, [Dār Kutub 'Ilmiyyah, Beirut, 1999/1419, 10+1 vols.]

Ibn Ḥajr, Shihābu-d-Dīn Aḥmad ibn 'Alī ibn Muḥammad

Fatḥ al-Bārī [Dār al-Kutub al-'Ilmiyyah, Beirut, 1st ed. 1989/1410, notes by 'Abdu-l-'Azīz ibn Bāz, 13+2 vols.]

Maṭālib al-'Āliyah [Dār al-Waṭan, Riyādh, 1st ed. 1997/1418, notes by Ghunaym ibn Ghunaym, 4+1 vols.]

Talkhīṣ al-Ḥabīr [Mu'assasah Qurṣuba, 1st ed. 1995/1416, 4 vols.]

Ibn Ḥibbān, Abū Ḥātim Muḥammad

Rawḍatu-l-'Uqalā [Dār ash-Sharīf, Riyādh, 2nd ed. 1997/1418, notes by Ibrāhīm al-Ḥāzimī]

Ṣaḥīḥ, [Mu'assasatu-l-Risālah, 2nd ed. 1997/1418, notes by Shu'ayb al-Arna'ūṭ, 16+2 vols.]

Ibn al-Jawzī, Abū-l-Farah 'Abdur-Raḥmān,

al-Mawḍū'āt [Dār al-Fikr, 2nd ed. 1983/1403, 3 vols.]

Ibn Kathīr, Abū al-Fiḍā' Ismā'īl,

al-Bidāyah wa-n-Nihāyah [Dār Iḥyā at-Turāth al-'Arabī, Beirut, 1993/1413, 14+1 vols.]

Ibn al-Qayyim, Shamsu-d-Dīn Abu 'Abdullāh Muḥammad

al-Fawā'id [Dār al-Kitāb al-'Arabī, Beirut, 5th Ed 1993/1414, notes by Muḥammad 'Uthmān]

Madārij as-Sālikīn [Dār al-Kitāb al-'Arabī, Beirut, 3 vols.]

Ibn Qutaybah,

Ta'wīl Mukhtalif al-Aḥādīth [Dār al-Kitāb al-'Arabī, Beirut]

Ibn Rajab, 'Abdur-Raḥmān ibn Aḥmad Zaynu-d-Dīn

Faḍl 'Ilm as-Salaf 'alā al-Khalaf [Dār 'Ammār, Ammān, 1st ed. 1986/1406, notes by 'Alī Ḥasan]

Faḍl 'Ilm as-Salaf 'alā al-Khalaf [Dār al-Arqam, Kuwait, 1st ed. 1983/1404, notes by Aḥmad an-Najmī]

Fatḥ al-Bārī Sharḥ Ṣaḥīḥ al-Bukhārī [Dār ibn al-Jawzī, 2nd ed. 1422, ed. Ṭ. 'Iwaḍullāh, 7 vols.]

al-Ḥākim, Abū 'Abdullāh Muḥammad ibn 'Abdullāh

al-Mustadrak 'alā as-Ṣaḥīḥayn [Dār al-Kutub al-'Ilmiyyah, Beirut, 1st ed.1990/1411, notes by Muṣṭapha 'Aṭā', 4+1 vols.]

al-Haythamī, Nūru-d-Dīn 'Alī ibn Abū Bakr

Majma' az-Zawā'id [Dār al-Kutub al-'Ilmiyyah, Beirut]

al-'Ijlūnī, Ismā'īl ibn Muḥammad,

Kashf al-Khafā' [Dār al-Kutub al-'Ilmiyyah, Beirut, 3rd ed. 1988/1408]

al-'Irāqī, Abū al-Faḍl Zayn ad-Dīn 'Abdur-Raḥīm,

al-Mughnī 'an Ḥamal al-Asfār [Dār at-Ṭabariyyah, 1st ed 1995/1415, notes Ashraf 'Abdu-l-Maqṣūd, 2+1 vols.]

al-Mubārakpūrī, Abū-l-'Alā Muḥammad 'Abdur-Raḥmān,

Tuḥfatu-l-Aḥwadhī Sharḥ Sunan at-Tirmidhī [Dār al-Kutub al-'Ilmiyyah, Beirut, 1st ed. 1990/1410, 10 vols.]

al-Munāwī, Muḥammad 'Abdur-Ra'ūf

Fayḍ al-Qadīr [Dār al-Kutub al-'Ilmiyyah, Beirut, 1st ed. 1994/1415, notes by Aḥmad 'Abdus-Salām, 6 vols.]

al-Nawawī, Yaḥyā ibn Sharaf,
Sharḥ Ṣaḥīḥ Muslim [Dār al-Kutub al-'Ilmiyyah, Beirut, 1st ed. 1995/1415, 18+1 vols.]
al-Sakhāwī, Muḥammad 'Abdur-Raḥmān,
Maqāṣid al-Ḥasanah [Dār al-Kitāb al-'Arabī, Beirut, 2nd ed. 1994/1414, ed. M. 'Uthmān]
al-Suyūṭī, Jalālu-d-Dīn 'Abdur-Raḥmān ibn Abū Bakr
ad-Durr al-Manthūr [Dār al-Kutub al-'Ilmiyyah, Beirut, 1st ed. 2000/1421, 6+1 vols.]
al-Lalī' al-Maṣnū'ah [Dār al-Kutub al-'Ilmiyyah, Beirut, 1st ed. 1996/1417, 2+1 vols.]
al-Ṭaḥāwī, Abū Ja'far Aḥmad ibn Muḥammad,
Sharḥ Mushkil al-Āthār [Mu'assasah ar-Risālah, Beirut, 1st ed. 1994/1415, ed. Shu'ayb al-Arna'ūṭ, 15+1 vols.]
al-Zurqānī, Muḥammad ibn 'Abdul-Bāqī,
Sharḥ Muwaṭṭa Mālik [Dār al-Kutub al-'Ilmiyyah, Beirut, 4 vols.]